No. 3023
$29.95

DESKTOP TYPOGRAPHY
WITH
QUARKXPRESS

FRANK J. ROMANO

Desktop Typography with QuarkXPress

Published by **Windcrest Books**
FIRST EDITION/SECOND PRINTING

Library of Congress Cataloging-in-Publication Data

Romano, Frank J.
    Desktop typography with QuarkXPress / by Frank Romano.
       p.   cm.
    Includes index.
    ISBN 0-8306-0223-2 ISBN 0-8306-9323-8 (pbk.)
     1. Desktop publishing. 2. QuarkXPress (Computer program)
3. Printing, Practical—Layout—Data processing. 4. Graphic arts-
-Data processing. I. Title.
Z286.D47R65 1988
686.'2—dc19

88-18129
CIP

TAB BOOKS Inc. offers software for sale. For information and a catalog, please contact TAB Software Department, Blue Ridge Summit, PA 17294-0850.

Questions regarding the content of this book should be addressed to:
Windcrest Books
Division of TAB BOOKS Inc.
Blue Ridge Summit, PA 17294-0850

Ron Powers: Director of Acquisitions

Desktop Typography with QuarkXPress

Table of Contents

Desktop Typography with QuarkXPress

A note on organization: The chapters that follow are self-contained. However, since many of the subjects overlap (for example, you'll find information about typefaces in several chapters) some material is repeated. Use the Index to find all of the pages that refer to a given topic.

 Information related specifically to QuarkXPress 2.0 is indented with the page symbol at left. All the typography and typographic examples were created via QuarkXPress 2.0. Illustrations were inserted using traditional methods.

The author wishes to thank Liz Bond at Adobe Systems for her help (only PostScript typefaces were used) and the people at Quark, Inc.

QuarkXPress is a registered trademark of Quark, Inc.

Introduction

Welcome to the world of type. This book was written to help novices and professionals understand and apply typographic principles.

Most of us grew up with a typewriter mentality. Many of our approaches to putting pages together evolved from pica and elite. "I want to bridge the gap between the typewriter and the printed page," said a typesetter in the 1870s. Since then, technological advances have brought the power to print to an ever-growing number of people.

In a little more than 100 years, the dreams of the 1870s have been realized. The birth of the personal computer coupled with the laser printer has placed typographic capability within reach of anyone who communicates with the printed or copied word. The infancy of desktop publishing was short and not altogether without problems.

Early desktop publishing programs violated many of the traditional applications of typography, and the pioneers who took the leap into PC publishing had to scramble to compensate for software deficiencies. One program that combines the standards of the past with the technology of the present is QuarkXPress.

Thus, when I was asked to develop a book on typography that could be used by QuarkXPress users to apply typography properly, I jumped at the chance.

Unlike many of the "How To" manuals adorning bookstore shelves these days, this book is not a re-hash of the QuarkXPress 2.0 reference manual. Rather, it is a training program about type using an excellent computer software program to demonstrate how typographic principles are applied. There are many aspects of QuarkXPress 2.0 that are not covered — importing and manipulating graphic images, and using color, for example, that are not discussed in this book.

The concentration is on type, in all its glory.

Frank Romano
Salem, New Hampshire

Chapter 1

Typography

What is typography? It is simply the use of type.

What is type? Type involves designed letterforms.

OK, what's a letterform? It's any letter or group of letters designed with common, repeating elements. Note how the characters below are related:

bdpqmnoc

The common design element is the bulbous, rounded serif at the beginning and at the ends of the strokes. The weight of the characters is consistent. There is a general look and feel that tie all the characters together. They represent a style of type, a *typeface*. Its uniqueness results from the special design of the letters of the alphabet.

That is the design of the letterform. *That* is type.

Type evolved from handwriting and the alphabet. The alphabet evolved as those who communicated in writing had to write faster.

Handwriting evolved from the needs of Phoenician merchants to keep records. The Greeks and Romans refined the alphabet, the primary conduit for communicating across the ages. How else could you think with Plato or calculate with Euclid or cry with Euripides?

In the eighth century A.D., Charlemagne standardized the written form of the alphabet and gave us the minuscule—our lowercase characters. Books were still the province of an elite few.

What is type?

Alphabet evolution

Evolution of the alphabet

Desktop Typography with QuarkXPress

During the Middle Ages, nameless monks and scribes scribbled their way to heaven preserving the thoughts and deeds of medieval civilization. Johann Gutenberg cast the letterform in metal and thrust the world into print communication. He opened the door for Martin Luther and Isaac Newton and Karl Marx.

Typewriter type vs. typographic type

While typographers often make the distinction between mono-spaced and proportionally spaced letterforms, both are type.

abcdefGHIJKL
Typewriter type (monospaced)

abcdefGHIJKL
Typographic type (proportionally spaced)

Typewriter letters all have the same width.

iiiii
wwwww
MMMMM
lllll

Typographically designed characters have different widths.

iiiii
wwwww
MMMMM
lllll

Variable word spaces

Note how the space between words in these paragraphs varies from line to line. These word spaces vary in width as needed for *justification*. The space between words is made narrower or wider to align text at the right margin. When lines of type are aligned with the left and right margins, it is called justification.

Therefore, with typographic type, you cannot use a word space as an indent, as you do on a typewriter. You cannot use a word space to align tabular copy, nor can you use it as a cursor control to move along a line as you can with a typewriter.

When you deal with typographic type instead of typewriter type, many of your page formatting habits change.

Type likes company. It is the stuff of which written communication is made. It is arranged in lines, paragraphs, and copy blocks. These elements form pages, which, in turn, form documents and publications. Each of the units builds on its predecessor.

Typography is concerned with the arrangement of type in lines and the spacing between characters, words, and lines. Consistency of spacing is one of the hallmarks of good typography.

This line has very erratic spacing between words

This line has consistent spacing between words

Typography is concerned with the the arrangement of the page, the positioning of blocks, the consistency of indention.

**Each line
has a different
    indent from the
left margin**

**Each line
has the same indent
from the left margin**

Typography is concerned with the characters and symbols that are used to communicate with the written word. See example below of a bullet and adjacent text.

- **This bullet is too small**
- **This one is better**

Typography *is* communication. Traditionally, typography falls under the broader heading of print communication. The reason is simple: usually, a number of units of the printed material are distributed, not just one. In most cases it is necessary to replicate or reproduce the page.

Typography is traditionalistic. Today's typographers follow time-honored rules that govern the relationship of letter to letter, letter to line, line to line, line to paragraph, paragraph to paragraph, paragraph to page, and page to page. Some rules are quite logical; others are not. Every rule can be broken, but usually at the expense of legibility, readability, and good typographic sense.

Consistent spacing

Typography is traditionalistic

Type is to be read

Typography is concerned with the typeface used for print communication and its appropriateness for the material. It is concerned with the size of the type and the length of the line.

TYPE IS MEANT TO BE READ
Type is meant to be read

You would not want type this big

for every line, or type this small for every line. Both are hard to read.

Type is meant to be read; it is designed to be read.

Tradition vs. innovation

Typography is flexible. There is ample opportunity for artistic expression. Good typography combines creativity and effective communication skills.

Creativity and pragmatism come together in typography. Type is only one of the many elements that can be used to produce a page. Lines, boxes, line art, photos, shapes, and color are all used to enhance print communication.

It is said that in art there are no rules. However, typographers must be concerned with the legibility of the characters they use and the effectiveness of the characters in communicating the textual message.

The challenge for any would-be publisher is to balance creativity and tradition when using type to produce a publication.

Typography: where the old meets the new; where tradition meets innovation. It is the heritage we receive from from the past and the legacy we pass on to the future.

Today's publishers are the inheritors of a tradition that goes back 500 years. Although technological advancements have led to the widespread use of electronic tools to produce pages, the fundamental processes of publishing are still very much the same as they were hundreds of years ago.

Chapter 2

Emphasis

Desktop Typography with QuarkXPress

Typography provides more opportunities for emphasizing information than typewriters or line printers. Typewriters and other monospaced printers have the following modes of presentation:

```
ALL CAPITAL LETTERS
ALL CAPITAL LETTERS UNDERLINED
Caps And Lowercase
Caps And Lowercase Underlined
```

On some computer-driven printers, the characters can be overstruck to create the appearance of bold, which gives us:

BOLD ALL CAPITAL LETTERS
BOLD ALL CAPITAL LETTERS UNDERLINED
Bold Caps And Lowercase
Bold Caps And Lowercase Underlined

There are many more opportunities for emphasis in typography :

Italic words and phrases
Bold words and phrases
Bold italic words and phrases
Outline words and phrases
Underlined plain text
~~Strike thru characters~~
Different fonts and sizes
. . . or variations of these

Emphasis should be used sparingly, usually for individual words and phrases. The essence of good typography is restraint. If you emphasize everything, then nothing is really emphasized.

The term "weight" refers to the lightness or darkness in print of a particular typeface based upon its design and thickness of line. There are many ways to vary the weight of type. The two most common versions are plain and **bold**.

Weight

The standard gradations of weight are:

- extra-light (also called hairline)
- light
- semi-light
- medium
- semi-bold
- bold
- extra-bold
- ultra-bold (also called "black")

Desktop Typography with QuarkXPress

The last two gradations are sometimes called "heavy" or "black." These terms are not standardized for example, a Helvetica Medium typeface may be the same weight as a Univers Bold. In typesetting, great care must be taken when determining whether a face is light, regular, medium, or bold because output engine density variations can affect image appearance. The supplier's name for the typeface may be totally arbitrary.

The most frequently used gradations are medium (also called "regular") and bold.

Bold

When marking a typewritten manuscript with typographic instructions, bold type is indicated by a wavy line under the copy. Recent technological developments have changed the boundaries of what was once called word processing. The process of markup is being reduced as word processing evolves to include typographic form.

Most typefaces have companion bold versions.

abcdefghijklmnopqrstuvwxyz
abcdefghijklmnopqrstuvwxyz

abcdefghijklmnopqrstuvwxyz
abcdefghijklmnopqrstuvwxyz

Note that the bold versions are wider than the plain versions. Usually, italic typeface widths are nearly equal to plain widths.

Variations in weight can occur, either intentionally or unintentionally, as a result of many factors. By varying the condition of processor chemicals, the length of processing time (fading), and the density setting on the phototypesetting machine itself, differences in weight may be artificially created. In some word processing situations, characters are struck twice to create a bold(er) look. The weight of characters printed by laserwriters also varies, depending on such variables as the age of the machine or the quality and age of the toner cartridge, and so on.

When trying to identify a particular typeface on a printed piece, you must consider the thickness or density of the ink, the amount of ink spread, and the number of photographic steps that the image went through before it made it to the printed page. Weight is harder to identify than style.

A bold lead-in, such as this, in which the first word or words of a paragraph are bold, should be in the same face and size as the text. If the lead-in is larger than the text, both should be baseline aligned.

Italic refers to the slant to the right of characters in a particular typeface. Italic type is a variation in posture of regular type.

Plain Type	Plain Type
Italic Type	*Italic Type*

Italic

In 1500 the *italic* typeface was developed. Manutius adapted the cursive handwriting used in the Papal Chancery and paid Francesco Griffo to cut punches in that style. At first the style was called "corsiva" (cursive) or "cancellarsca" (chancery). Sometimes it was called the "Italian hand." In Germany, "Kursiv" means "italic." Like the word "roman," the word "italic" credits Italy as the land of origin. The term, however, was coined by the French and was not capitalized.

Manutius did not intend italic for emphasis, which is its primary use today. He had the typeface cut because it was narrower than the roman typeface. He could get more italic words on a page, and he was able to produce books that looked more professional and could be sold at a lower price. Later, roman (that is, non-italic) styles were modified to be narrower and more legible. Because italic text was too hard to read, italic never became a standard typeface.

Robert Granjon, who worked for Garamond, the first type-founder, cut about 10 styles for Christopher Plantin of Antwerp (1520-89). One of these became the model for an italic style designed as a *companion* to a roman style (called a *sympathetic* italic). It was a different style, closer to handwriting than the roman, and the letters appeared to be linked.

Kinds of italics

There are three kinds of italics.

- *Unrelated* italics are "pure" styles based on fifteenth-century "hands." There is no corresponding roman face.

- *Related* italics are designed to complement a specific roman typeface but are still more or less "pure" italic.

- *Matching* italics are essentially the same design as a particular roman typeface. Digitized typesetting devices that modify characters electronically to create the italic are creating matching italics, although purists will call them "oblique" or "slant."

Although the slant of the italic will vary, an accepted standard is 78 degrees. Italic type is now used for emphasis, titles, quotations, and extracts. Most of these items were once set in small caps, but the limitations of machine typesetting and the advent of photographic typesetting did them in. Recently, there has been a renaissance in the use of small caps, and italic should be allowed to return to its proper use: emphasis.

Certain characters may change form when they make the transition from roman to italic:

abcdefghijklmnopqrstuvwxyz
abcdefghijklmnopqrstuvwxyz

abcdefghijklmnopqrstuvwxyz
abcdefghijklmnopqrstuvwxyz

Look at the lowercase a and r in the plain and italic type examples above. Most characters are changed to some extent by the type designer. Merely slanting plain characters could not accomplish the changes you see in the examples above. The lowercase f is usually most affected.

f *f*   f *f*   f *f*
Times   **Garamond**   **Palatino**

Tilting vs. true italic

Tilting plain characters to the left (backslant) or right (oblique) is called "slant." This kind of distortion is now done by digitized printers and typesetters, and the characters created are not the same as true italic.

As far as typography is concerned, the terms "italic," "cursive," and "oblique" all mean the same thing: the slanted version of a given typeface. Italic is still the preferred term in English-speaking countries and in France.

Most other countries, however, use the term "cursive," which means running or flowing. The term "oblique" was most commonly associated with the Futura or sans serif family of typefaces. Below is an example of News Gothic, a geometric sans (without) serif typeface:

abcdefghijklmnopqrstuvwxyz
abcdefghijklmnopqrstuvwxyz

In the case of the Futura typeface, oblique was used rather than italic or cursive because the designer, Paul Renner, felt that the Futura italic was not a "true" italic and that it should have a name that more accurately described it. So he called it "oblique," by which he simply meant slanted. Many sans serif styles were created in this manner.

A general rule for using slanted type: Sans serif typefaces may be slanted; serif typefaces should not be slanted under penalty of torture.

In markup, italic is indicated by an underline under the copy. Quotation marks and underlining are alternatives to italic for highlighting or emphasizing text. All-capital italic lines should be avoided.

The most common copy to be put in italic:

What to put in italic

- titles of publications
- names of ships, trains, aircraft
- unfamiliar foreign words and phrases
- scientific names
- mathematical unknowns
- protagonists in legal citations
- words quoted by name
- quotations
- names of shows or plays (see next page for italicizing TV shows)

Italicize unfamiliar foreign words and phrases (but not whole sentences) appearing in English text. Exceptions: use roman type, the standard typeface, for all foreign titles preceding proper names and for names of foreign institutions whose significance prevents any translation into English words.

Use roman and quotes for all titles of articles taken from foreign-language journals and chapter headings.

Desktop Typography with QuarkXPress

You should also italicize:

- titles of books and essays
- plays and motion pictures
- symphonies and operas
- a poem long enough to appear as a book
- pamphlets, published documents
- newspapers, periodicals, and journals
- the words *Journal, Review*, etc., when standing alone if they are a part of the name of the publication
- titles of unpublished matter
- titles of parts of published works
- titles of book series
- radio and television series (use quotes for individual episodes)
- short musical compositions
- books of the Bible, canonical and apocryphal
- titles of ancient manuscripts; all symbols used to designate manuscripts should be set in roman type
- Latin words, phrases, and abbreviations as used in literary and legal references
- names of plaintiff and defendant in the citation of legal cases; also the titles of proceedings containing such prefixes as *in re, ex parte*, and *in the matter of*, etc.
- the title added to a person's name (in signatures only). If the title consists of only one word, it is run into the same line with the name; if it is more than one word, but no longer than the name, center the first letter under the name line and indent one em space on the right. If the added title is longer than the name, center the name over the second line and set flush.
- letters, such as *a), b), c),* used to indicate subdivisions (single parenthesis when beginning a paragraph, double parentheses if run in); *a, b, c,* etc., when affixed to the number of a verse, page, or another reference figure, to denote a fractional part; and *a* and *b,* when used with page numbers to indicate left and right columns of text
- letters used to designate unknown quantities, lines, etc., in algebraic, geometrical, and scientific matter
- numbers in legends or in text that refer to corresponding letters or numbers in accompanying illustrations, whether or not they are in italics with the illustration

Do not italicize:

> • cf., e.g., etc., viz., v. or vs. (versus). Italicize *See* and *See also* when used for cross-reference in an index, and *for* and *read* in a list of errata. In both cases the need to distinguish the significant words calls for a reversal of the normal practice for emphasis.

Exceptions: Some rules may be disregarded in extensive bibliographical lists, in tables, or in other matter in which their use would result in an undue preponderance of italics.

Bold italic is used infrequently for subheads or advertising applications. It is available with almost every font, since fonts usually come with four versions:

> • Plain or normal
> • *Italic (refers to the plain italic)*
> • **Bold**
> • ***Bold italic***

You can also underline type characters, which is actually a contradiction. Underlining was originally used in typewriting for emphasis and to indicate the equivalent of italic. Some people think that underlining typographic characters is a common practice. It is not. Underlining should be a design decision, and creativity should never override clarity.

Technically, when underlining text the underline should run behind the descending characters; it should not go through them (as in the first example below).

yuppie   yuppie

Typographic emphasis is useful for breaking up copy blocks to relieve unbroken grayness. Used properly and with restraint, bold and italic type can give style and emphasis to words in print.

Here are several examples of subheads and text lead-ins:

This is a slightly larger italic lead-in for this block. The size was increased from 12-point to 18-point.

Larger sized lead-in, italic type

What not to put in italic

Bold italic

Underline

Copy block emphasis

More subheads and lead-ins

HERE is bold italic used at the same size. In this case small caps were used for the first word to give it additional emphasis.

Small cap lead-in, bold italic type

This is a subhead
Subheads are often given emphasis and should be treated consistently within a publication.

Bold head, same size, same leading as text

This is a subhead
Subheads are often given emphasis and should be treated consistently within a publication.

Bold italic head, same size, same leading as text

This is a subhead
Subheads are often given emphasis and should be treated consistently within a publication.

Bold head, same size, same leading as text; head indented

This is a subhead
Subheads are often given emphasis and should be treated consistently within a publication.

Bold head, same size, same leading as text; both indented

This is a subhead

Subheads are often given emphasis and should be treated consistently within a publication.

Bold head, same size, extra leading

This is a subhead
Subheads are often given emphasis and should be treated consistently within a publication.

Bold head, larger point size than text

This is a subhead

Subheads are often given emphasis and should be treated consistently within a publication.

Bold sans serif head, larger point size than text

This is a subhead

     Subheads are often given emphasis and should be treated consistently within a publication.

Bold head, same size, same leading as text; text indented

This is a subhead

_____Subheads are often given emphasis and should be treated consistently within a publication.

Bold head, same size, same leading as text; rule line indent

Even more subheads and lead-ins

Chapter 3

Columns

Type is set in lines. The width of a line (also called column width, line length, or measure) refers to its horizontal length.

Traditionally, line length meant the area between two margins. But margins refer to page characteristics, not always to line characteristics. Thus, line length is the width of the line on which you will place type. To achieve maximum readability, it is wise to consider a few time-tested rules regarding column widths.

Line length is measured in picas and points. Most often, typographers measure line lengths in whole number picas or half picas (for example, 13.6 describes a line that is 13 and a half picas long, since there are 12 points to a pica). You can, of course, makes columns any length within reason.

Line length

Sometimes the formula *Font size $\times$ 2* is used to determine the maximum line length. *Lowercase alphabet $\times 1.5$* is also used.

According to the first formula, 9-point type $\times$ 2 = 18, meaning that 18 picas (3 inches) is the maximum line length you should use with 9-point type. To determine line length using the second formula, type the lowercase alphabet in the style and size that will be used for the text:

abcdefghijklmnopqrstuvwxyz

Then measure it with a pica ruler. Multiply that number by 1.5. The concept is that alphabet length is based on the overall width of the characters of the face and thus can serve as a basis for determining line length. Wider faces look best with wider line lengths; condensed faces look best with narrow line lengths.

A line with 55 to 60 characters (9 to 10 words) provides optimum readability. Also, as a line length increases, paragraph indentations should increase, too.

Narrow columns are best

Double or multiple columns with narrow line lengths are preferable to wide columns. Research about the readability of varying line lengths (most of it by Professors Tinker and Patterson) concluded that lines having 55 to 60 characters provide optimum readability. The most important consideration when determining line length is legibility. If you use a clear and easy-to-read type, 55 to 60 characters will be fine. If the type is small, or harder to read, reduce the line length.

Desktop Typography with QuarkXPress

Saccadic jumps

We read by taking in a grouping of characters, called a saccad. The more times we have to jump from saccad to saccad, the harder it is to read a line.

This is an example of how eye (saccadic) movements may progress during reading. Circles indicate the focusing points for each stop (fixation), while the squares show the approximate area covered by the eye during a fixation. Broken lines indicate saccadic jumps, and solid lines are (re-reading) regressions.

Saccadic jumps

If you discover that a one-column format will result in lines that are too wide, change to a two- or three-column format. Actually, for 8.5-inch-wide paper, you are virtually forced to use a multi-column format to achieve optimum readability. This is not to say that judicious white space is a bad thing—just don't overdo it.

Type mass

Another important factor is the type mass itself. A group of 12 to 15 lines of type set at a 48-pica (48 picas is about 8 inches) line measure looks fine. That's due to the small amount of type. A full page with a 48-pica column set in 10-point type is extremely tiring for a reader. Such a large type mass tends to blur, making the page look like one large gray blob. There's little for the eye to grab onto.

If possible, use more than one line length—that way, the eye gets a little variety. You can also break up gray areas with hanging indents, subheads, lists, or other diversions. Such emphasis also provides visual cues to the important points.

Other ways of achieving visual diversity are:

- paragraph indents
- extra space between paragraphs
- indented blocks or paragraphs, left, right, or both
- lists like this, bulleted or otherwise
- notches or insets for illustrations

Blocks of indented type and blocks of type used with illustrations are called notches or insets.

A left notch Some PC publishing programs, particularly QuarkXPress, let you add illustrations or photographs within columns of text. An inserted graphic that doesn't span the column is called an inset, and some programs will run text around insets.

Copy that goes around an inset is called a **A right notch** runaround or a wrap. The line length for runaround text should should be equal (in picas) to the point size of the type. For example, 10-point type requires at least a 10-pica line length.

 You can create indented paragraphs (left indented, right indented or left and right indented) with the indent functions of QuarkXPress. Select the **Formats** menu command under the **Style** menu. Then enter the indent values in the appropriate text fields of the **Paragraph Formats** dialog box.

Creating runarounds in QuarkXPress

Indents usually restrict you to square or rectangular insets. However, you can also create irregularly shaped indents using QuarkXPress's box and oval creation tools. You simply draw the shape you want and place it so text runs around the shape. You can also automatically run type around scanned images of any shape.

The decision between creating indents using the **Paragraph Formats** functions or the graphic tools depends on the page you are creating. If the inset illustration is to stay in one place on the page with copy running around it, use the graphic tool. However, if the illustration must stay with the copy, use the indent functions. In the latter case, you could wind up with part of the indented copy on one page and part on another. Keep in mind also that you may have to manually move the illustration to keep it in its proper place if you change the position of the accompanying text.

If you are setting a 13-pica column in 10-point type and you want to insert a half-column illustration, the "optimum" line length for the runaround should be 10 picas. You can break this rule, but be careful not to create narrow line lengths that are too narrow. Narrow columns can result in erratic word spacing.

Remember, an inset in a narrow column will create an even narrower line length for the type. Try to balance the size of the object with the width of the column.

Desktop Typography with QuarkXPress

Formatting copy blocks

You have four choices when formatting copy blocks: ragged right, which is the standard typewriter format, ragged left, ragged center, and justified.

Ragged copy

This paragraph is set ragged right. Notice that there is no hyphenation. Copy blocks without hyphenation often have erratic line lengths—some are long, others are short.

Ragged right, no hyphenation

This paragraph is set ragged right. Notice that it is hyphenated. Hyphenating copy results in more consistent line lengths.

Ragged right, with hyphenation

This paragraph is set ragged left. Note that there's no hyphenation. Without it the lines are long and short, quite erratic.

Ragged left, no hyphenation

This paragraph is set ragged center. Note that there is no hyphenation. Without it the lines are long and short, quite erratic.

Ragged center, no hyphenation

To hyphenate or not to hyphenate

Ragged type can be hyphenated or not hyphenated. Usually, hyphenation results in more even-looking blocks; however, if line lengths are too even, it looks like poor justification.

It is preferable not to hyphenate proper names. Most advertising copy blocks are ragged right, without hyphenation.

Use ragged center if you do invitations or special display work. Don't use it for text.

In addition to the aforementioned ragged formats, text blocks can also be justified. Justification means that all lines are exactly the same length, which results in square blocks of copy. Justification is accomplished by fitting as many words (or parts of words when using hyphenation) on a line as possible and adding white space (between words, characters, or both) to make the last letter align with the right margin. Because word spaces vary in justified copy, a word space cannot be used as an indent or positioning element.

Although you can specify certain limitations for word spaces, you are at the mercy of the words on the line and the ability of the program you are using to hyphenate at the most advantageous (and correct) places.

Many studies have been done to determine whether justified or ragged-right text is easier to read. The results give a slight edge to ragged right. The reasoning is that the space between words is consistent and words are generally not hyphenated as they are in justified text.

Spacing between words should be uniform to assist the reader in identifying word shapes. If the space between words is too narrow, the copy tends to run together. Words that are spaced too far apart are also hard to read. Proper word spacing helps the reader to recognize words easily.

Word spacing varies in justified text. Some programs allow you to set values for:

- desired or optimum word space
- minimum word space that's acceptable
- maximum word space before hyphenation can occur

All values for word spacing should be adjustable. Some programs justify type using hyphenation and variable word spacing, while others vary the letterspacing to achieve justification. The latter process should be avoided under penalty of torture.

Justification

Variable word spaces

Chapter 4

Type Size

The basic unit of measurement in typography is the *point*. All other dimensions and terms used in printing derive from this unique measurement. The *point* is used to describe the size of typefaces, line spacing, and other elements of composition, but it also leads to great confusion. The growth of printing technology has fostered several incompatible systems for measuring type, all based on the *point* but none having a *point* of equal size.

In North America and Britain the point is approximately 1/72nd of an inch (.351mm) and is called the *pica point*. In Europe the point is slightly larger (.376mm) and is called the *Didot point*. The ratio of these two units is 7:5.5.

Points have always been used to measure the size of a chunk of metal type. A 72-point H, in metal type, is a character cast onto the top of a one-inch-high (72-point) metal block. The block carries the letter through all the printing operations. The actual impression or image height of the H when printed is smaller than the size of the metal block that holds it. Traditionally, the point size of type refers to specific dimension of the metal and *not* to

The point

The legacy of metal type

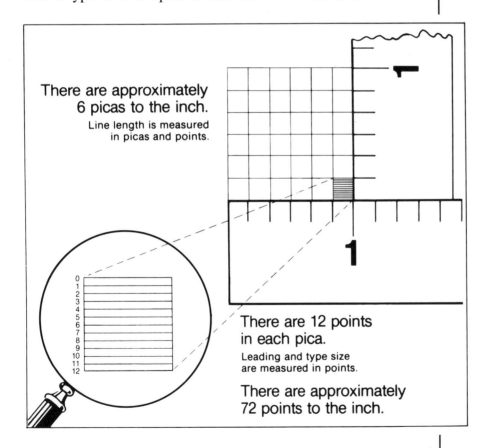

There are approximately
6 picas to the inch.

Line length is measured
in picas and points.

There are 12 points
in each pica.

Leading and type size
are measured in points.

There are approximately
72 points to the inch.

image height. All of the H's below are 24-point, but you can see the difference in their height:

H **H** H *H*

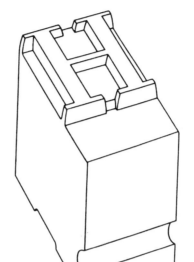

Metal type

This discrepancy is necessary because of the *ascenders* and *descenders*. If the type was to line up squarely and securely, each character had to have been cast onto an oversized metal block that is large enough to allow for these extremes of projection above and below the baseline. Thus, all the metal blocks used for a typeface ended up being equal in height, and this height is what determines the point size of the typeface.

Standardization of the point system

For centuries, there was no system for comparing (in the same measurement units) two typefaces of different size. Each individual size had a name, not a number (for example, Diamond, Brevier, Pica and Great Primer were sizes, not styles). Typefaces could not be related quantitatively to faces slightly larger and slightly smaller in size.

In the late 1800s, the typographic industry adopted the point system that had been developed in France a century earlier by Pierre Fournier. Adoption of the point system has resulted in better descriptions of metal size as well as the vertical spacing between lines of type, but it has left other matters unresolved.

Point size was originally an expression of the distance from the top of an ascender to the bottom of a descender (plus a little bit of space above and below for the metal *shoulder*) and, as such, could not describe the proportional relationship between a typeface's x-height (the height of the lowercase letter *x)* and its ascenders and descenders.

Take a close look at pages containing different 24-point type-faces (e.g. Helvetica vs. Garamond vs. Times). You will notice that they look very different. Since the x-height of a typeface has the greatest effect on its appearance, a 60-point face with short ascenders and descenders will have a much greater visual impact than a similar-sized type with long ascenders and descenders. All three of the faces below are 24-point, yet notice how much larger the Helvetica type seems by virtue of its greater x-height.

Point size variations

Garamond Helvetica Times

The usefulness of the point in describing line spacing and the like cannot be denied. When dealing with very small type, it is preferable to deal in round numbers (rather than fractions of inches or millimeters). The result has been a far greater selection of typefaces, but even further complication in describing the height of a specific letter. A font of "24-point" letters may have been adapted from hot type 24 *pica* points high, hot type 24 *Didot* points high, or from photolettering that has a tenuous point designation. It may even have been originally designed for pho-totype, in which case the capital letters might be 24 points high (pica *or* Didot).

The traditional point measurements associated with hot type are a hindrance in the world of photo and laser type. Very little of the type composed these days is created with metal slugs. Instead, it is created directly on a sheet of paper or film. It would be easy to change to a system using actual letter image heights. This would be a much more logical way to exploit the special attributes of digital type. The height of a capital H could simply be expressed in points or, perhaps, millimeters.

Originally, type size referred to the individual piece of metal that held each character. The character casters and linecasters did not change this approach. For many years, type size was a constant measurement and only the x-height varied. Since there were few sizes cast for faces at that time, it was not a difficult task to learn to identify sizes on sight.

Clash of tradition and technology

The advent of photographic typesetting changed all that. Two divergent approaches developed. The first was that of *photolet-tering,* which referred to headline and display work. The master size on the photo matrix was usually one inch (72-point), and all enlargements and reductions modified this basic size. Thus, the concept of standard type sizes was lost because one could specify any size height or width necessary to fit a layout. The previously used increments of 6, 7, 8, etc. were meaningless in photolettering.

Phototypesetting

Then came *phototypesetting,* or more accurately, *phototextsetting*, and three techniques were used for type sizing.

1. Each photo matrix had a different master size and characters were photographed 1:1.
2. The photo matrix had one master size, 8-point for example, and lenses enlarged or reduced the character image.
3. The photo matrix included a variety of master sizes, and each size was enlarged to create a range of sizes. For example, an 8-point master could be used for enlargements up to 12 points. At that point, a 12-point master was used for 12-point type and enlargements up to 18 points, and so on.

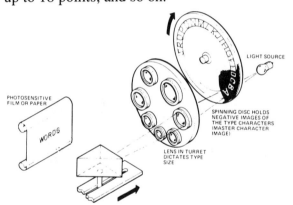

A typical optical sizing system for phototypesetting

Some suppliers standardized their master sizes and worked from uniformly sized artwork. Thus, all original typeface art would be 7 inches; it would then be reduced to the 8-point master size. In many cases this effectively eliminated the x-height variability between typefaces. All sizes were simply enlargements or reductions of a standard size.

Digital type

In newer digitized printing and typesetting, the image is not a photographic master. It is made up of thousands of dots, overlapped to create lines (called rasters). Thus, the number of type sizes is increasing.

Desktop Typography with QuarkXPress

The growth of type sizes:

1. Hot metal limited the number of type sizes because of the sheer weight of carrying a face in too many sizes.
2. Size-for-size photo matrices also limited the number of sizes available because the typesetting device could not hold very many masters to begin with.
3. The lens machines were at first limited by the number of lenses that could fit in the turret. The development of zoom lens machines gave an extended range.
4. Digitized printers and typesetters create sizes electronically and can create an almost infinite size range.

- Hot metal—15 to 20 sizes from 6 to 72 point.
- Photo (size for size)—20 to 25 sizes, 6 to 72 point.
- Photo (lens turret)—12 to 20 sizes, $5^{1}/2$ to 72 point.
- Photo (zoom lens)—50 to 140 sizes, $5^{1}/2$ to 74 point.
- Digital—200 to 500 sizes, 5 to 130 point.
- Advanced digital—1,000 to 10,000 sizes, 5 to 500 point.

Notice how small the increments below are:

Varying point sizes

24.00 POINT
24.25 POINT
24.50 POINT
24.75 POINT
25.00 POINT
25.25 POINT
25.50 POINT
25.75 POINT
26.00 POINT

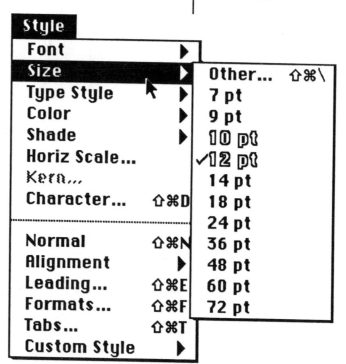

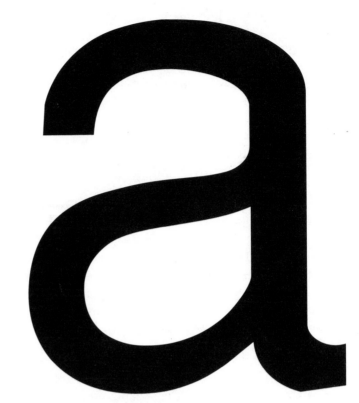

This is a 500-point character.

This is a 5-point character.

Limit the number of point sizes you use

Some of the most beautiful typography ever done has been set in one or two sizes using one or two typefaces. It's nice to have thousands of sizes available, but use them judiciously.

Keep the number of point sizes in a job to a minimum. Usually there are definable elements that vary in point size:

- **Text.** This comprises 80 percent of the material. Choose a readable size for the text font, usually between 9-point and 12-point. The two most popular text sizes are 9-point and 10-point.

- **Subheads.** There are two ways to set subheads: run-in subheads are set on the same line as the text; other subheads are set a line above the text. Both styles are used to break up text blocks. The trend is to set sub-heads in the same size as the text with a variation in weight. Subheads that are on lines by themselves can be set either larger or smaller than the text, but it's preferable to set both elements in the same size.

- **Chapter heads.** These are usually the largest characters on a page. The chapter number or section number could be larger than the chapter head.

- **Section heads.** Section heads should be slightly larger than the subheads.

- **Footnotes.** Traditionally, footnotes are between 6-point and 9-point. There are rules governing the size of footnote and text type in certain legal, banking, insurance, and contract forms. In most cases, a minimum of 10-point type is required with one point of leading.

- **Extracts:** Usually, extracts are the same size as the text with indents on one or both sides. For publications with many long extracts, it is acceptable to reduce the size by one or two points.

- **Advertising.** Most advertisements have a large head, possibly a subhead, and a block of text. However, the sizes can vary widely. The tendency is to set the head in the largest size that the copy will allow and vice versa.

QuarkXPress lets you specify type sizes between 2 and 500 points in quarter-point increments—almost 2,000 sizes. This provides a capability similar to photolettering in that a precise size (10.75 points, for example) can be selected for a specific use.

Sizing type in QuarkXPress

In QuarkXPress, point size is specified using the **Size** sub-menu command in the **Style** menu. Popular sizes and those that have screen fonts are listed. You can use the **Other** menu command in the **Size** sub-menu to specify any point size. You can also access the font size dialog box rapidly by keying **Shift-Command-**

Chapter 5

Fonts

Your typewriter or word processor keytops are the visual representation of a *font*. Each key is etched with the character or symbol it can print out when the key is struck. If the font element on the printout device can be changed, there may be alternative "layouts" with a different set of characters and symbols.

A font is a set of characters in a particular typeface. Sometimes the definition is used to describe the characters in one style and also in one point size. This occurred because there was no automated method for "manufacturing" various sizes from one master set. Today, most systems let you specify size; thus, font refers to the typeface style only.

Typewriter vs. typographic font

```
!@#$%^&*()_+
1234567890-=
QWERTYUIOP
qwertyuiop[]
ASDFGHJKL:"
asdfghjkl;'
ZXCVBNM,.?
zxcvbnm,./
```

```
1234567890=`¡™£¢∞§¶•ªº–≠
!@#$%^&*()_+¤‹›fifl‡°·‚—±
QWERTYUIOP{}|œΣ´®†¥¨^øπ""
qwertyuiop[]ASDFGHJKL:"
åß∂ƒ©˙∆˚¬…æÅÍÎÏÌÓÔÒÚÆ
ZXCVBNM<>?ÛÙÇ◊ı~˜zxcvb
```

Typewriter font

Typographic font

The term "wrong font" or "w.f." refers to an incorrect character or **group** of characters (like the preceding word, "group," set in Helvetica instead of Times). This was a common problem when operators used blind keyboards and could not see font representation on the screen.

A type font contains *all* of the alphanumerics, punctuation marks, special characters, ligatures, and symbols that

Gutenberg's font had 292 characters and combinations of characters so that it could emulate handwriting.

are contained in *one given version* of a typeface. The term "alphanumeric" refers to any letter or numeral.

The same fonts from different manufacturers may not have the same special characters:

- One version may provide a # and @, while the other may provide an asterisk or a bullet.
- A third version may have all of these symbols.
- There might also be differences in design, weight, and even point size. Thus, a font may contain a complete set of complementary special characters or it may be used with a variety of pi or symbol fonts in order to create complementary characters.

Also, in mark-up it is important to specify a font by its full and correct name: Helvetica Extra Bold Extended (or Helv. X-Bold Ext.) to prevent typesetting the wrong font.

Watch for punctuation style

- Periods, commas, colons, and semicolons are set in the typeface (italic or bold) of the preceding word. A single italic letter preceding any punctuation mark does not require setting the mark in italic type.

    Good-night, sweet prince!
    Good-night, sweet prince!

- Set quotation marks, exclamation marks, and question marks according to the overall context of the sentence.

- Parentheses and brackets are set according to the overall context of the sentence regardless of the typeface within them. Italic parenthetical expressions standing alone take italic parentheses.

    (Italic text with regular parentheses.)
    (Italic text with italic parentheses.)

- Italic parenthetical expressions following a head (in any typeface) would take medium (light) weight roman parentheses, except the word *continued*, which would take italic parentheses.

Fonts are part of a typeface series:

Type family:	Helvetica
Typeface:	Helvetica Light Condensed (weight and width)
Type size:	10-point Helvetica Light Condensed
Type font:	Helvetica Light Condensed
	with a job layout of 96 characters
Type series:	6- to 18-point Helvetica Light Condensed
	with a job layout of 96 characters

There are several variables that affect the output of type:

- **Master.** The master image may be modified for the technical considerations of the device.
- **Outputting.** The output device, in the process of outputting, may create variation.
- **Processing.** The development of the image by photographic means or the use of newer technologies can affect the resultant image. The output of laser printers, for example, varies depending on toner quality and density.
- **Operator Control.** Deliberate changes in density, weight, width, size, or position by the operator.

With so many variables, it is no wonder that type cannot be matched precisely.

Roman type is an all-encompassing term for typefaces based upon the *serif* variations developed by the ancient Romans and further developed by Italian humanistic lettering.

Roman type

H H **H** H

Today, typographers use the term roman to indicate the main typeface in a family of typefaces. A family could include, for example, roman, italic, bold, and bold italic typefaces. In some instances, typeface names are accompanied by "roman" titles—"Times Roman" and "Century Roman," for example. Sans serif faces should not be designated as roman. Although you may hear "Helvetica Roman," this is a contradiction in terms because Helvetica is a sans serif typeface.

There were a number of "inspirations" for the roman typeface:

The evolution of the roman typeface

ABCDEF

The first and foremost was the roman capital, as illustrated by the inscription on Trajan's Column in Rome.

LONCIUS

The uncial and early Blackletter variations of the roman caps.

CDOYTUIC

The Caroline minuscules—the "standardized" hand sponsored by Charlemagne.

Moyſes naſcitur

The typefaces of Nicholas Jenson and Manutius of Venice as used in *Eusebius*.

The faces of Claude Garamond, William Caslon, John Baskerville, and Giambatista Bodoni also added to the evolution of the roman typeface.

The "Trajan letter" shapes, cut into the stone panel 10 feet above the ground in the pedestal of the column, are considered perfect roman-proportioned forms and still guide type designers. They are not all the same size because they were created using a variety of lines graduated in height to make the characters look the same to the viewer on the ground.

Compare the roman typefaces below. Note the relationship of thick and thin elements.

Gpx

Old Style: a characteristic style of roman typefaces typified by very little differentiation between thicks and thins, diagonal stress, capitals shorter than ascenders and serifs that are small and graceful. The sample is Garamond.

Transitional: a characteristic style of roman typefaces between Old Style and Modern, typified by sharper thick/thin contrast, sharper and thinner serif endings. Baskerville is the sample.

Gpx

Gpx

Modern: a characteristic style of roman typeface typified by vertical stress, hairline serifs, and maximum contrast between thicks and thins. The sample is Bodoni.

 *Square:* also called "Egyptian" and usually characterized by the uniform weight of the stem and the serif. Lubalin Graph is the sample.

There are also novelty serifs that defy description.

Serif is an all-inclusive term for characters that have a line crossing the free end of a stroke. It is said that the Romans invented the serif as a solution to the technical problem of getting a chisel to cut a neat, clean end to a stroke.

Trajan Column type

Later serifs became an emulation of handwriting with flat "pens" that produced thick and thin curves.

Certainly, serif characters increase readability by providing a horizontal guideline for the eye that "ties" the letters of words together. It is generally better to use serif faces when typesetting long blocks of copy, such as books, because serif faces cause less eye fatigue.

The most common types of serifs are shown below:

H H H H

Bodoni   Lubalin   Korinna   Garamond

Thin (or Hairline)   Square (or Slab)   Round   Cupped

Characters without serifs are called *sans serif.* Such characters were originally called "grotesque." In the United States, the term "gothic" was sometimes used as a synonym for sans serif. Although serif type is easier to read in text, sans serif is generally easier to read in headlines.

Desktop Typography with QuarkXPress

Sans serif | Below are three popular sans serif typefaces:

Hag
Helvetica

Hag
News Gothic

Hag
Avant Garde

In the 1920s Paul Renner created a typeface called Futura. It was based upon geometric shapes and influenced by the Bauhaus, a German training school for architects and designers that was founded in 1919 by the architect, Walter Gropius. Futura would influence the next generation of type designers who developed sans serif typefaces, such as Univers and Helvetica.

Futura Book   *Futura Book Italic*

Futura

Grotesque

Grotesque is a generic term used to describe sans serif faces. The word first appeared in 1832 when William Thorowgood, in a supplement to his type specimen book, showed an unseriffed design that he named "Grotesque."

In the period between the two world wars, the British Monotype Corporation created, as its fourth typeface, an alphabet of unseriffed capitals. Meanwhile, the Germans were philosophizing about letters without serifs. The principal catalyst was the Bauhaus. The basic principle in all Bauhaus work was "functionalism"—simple, clinical forms without decorations. To the typographer, this translated into letterforms uncluttered by serifs or variations in stroke width.

The Bauhaus and its philosophies had a profound influence on the United States and Switzerland. The Swiss "Graphiker's" (graphic designer's) fine use of grotesque faces and the excellence of the Swiss presswork were fundamental to the success of these faces. They became even more popular after the 1928 publication of Jan Tschichold's innovative book, *"Die Neue Typographie,"* which was set in a light grotesque. In fact, grotesques were used so extensively by the Swiss (Max Bill was one of the major trendsetters) that the "New Typography" eventually became known as "Swiss Typography."

In the 1950s, the most popular grotesques were the Monotype 215 and 216 series, which typified fine "Swiss Typography." Designers, using 215 and 216 mainly as text faces, combined them with display sizes of Neue Haas Grotesque, which later developed into Helvetica. In the United States these faces were called "gothic," "grotesque," and "gro-gothic" for many years. These terms aren't used much any more, though they may be found in typefaces with such names as "News Gothic" and "Trade Gothic."

G g

Example of gothic type (News Gothic)

G g

Example of other sans serif type (Helvetica)

GOTHIC

IS A MISLEADING NAME

NOT AN OUTGROWTH OF BLACK-LETTER

IT IS A RUDE IMITATION OF THE EARLIEST FORMS OF ROMAN LETTER CUT IN STONE

THIS FACE OF TYPE

IS KNOWN IN GREAT BRITAIN AS

GROTESQUE

IT IS THE SIMPLEST FORM
OF LETTER, WITH STROKES
NEARLY UNIFORM IN THEIR
THICKNESS, AND WITHOUT
SERIFS, FOR WHICH REASON
IT IS SOMETIMES CALLED

SANS-SERIF

Even in 1900 the terms were in contention.

In any case, they are all sans serif.

Chapter 6

Placement

Quadding

In typography, type must be placed on lines and the lines must be placed on pages. Quadding is the traditional term for placement. The word is a shortened form of "quadrat," a blank cube of metal used for filling blank space in handset type. All type had to "lock up." This meant that lines with only one word on them had to be filled with non-printing blanks. The blanks, or quads, "positioned" the type.

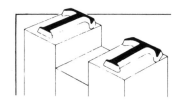

This is one view of what a quad (center block) looked like

QUAD RIGHT

QUAD LEFT

QUAD CENTER

QUAD MIDDLE

This is another, more conceptual view of what quads look like

Linecasters mechanized the process with semiautomatic attachments that filled the blank areas of a line with metal. These "quadders" were either mechanized, electric, or hydraulic. The popularity of the hydraulic method led to the use of the term "flush" as a verb for positioning. Today, "flush" and "quad" are used interchangeably.

The function of quadding always takes place on the baseline between the pre-set margins that determine line length:

The term "quad lock" describes the function of repetitive quadding to the same position. Thus, a "quad center lock" means that every line (actually every item ending with a return) will be centered. Text blocks set ragged left, right, and center are actually created with quad locks.

Desktop Typography with QuarkXPress

Paragraph indent

Indention (sometimes mistakenly called "indentation") is a form of placement for text and display showing the relation of items, one to another.

The simplest indent is the *paragraph*, which denotes the beginning of a text block. A paragraph indent should be proportional to the line length:

- under 24 picas — 1 em space (2 en spaces)
- 25–36 picas — 1.5 em spaces (3 en spaces)
- 37 picas or more — 2 em spaces (4 en spaces)

It should be noted that an em space is equal in width to the point size being used. If run-in subheads or initial caps are larger than the text, a 1-em indent will be the same size as the first character. When indenting text blocks, you should make sure that paragraph indents are set to the size of the body text and not to the size of the subhead or initial cap:

| This line is indented one em space at the left.

| This line is also indented one em space, but it is based on the size of the initial cap. Note that the space is slightly wider than the space in the sentence above.

A *hanging* indent is the opposite of the paragraph indent. When hanging indents are used, the first line of a paragraph is set to the full line measure; subsequent lines in the paragraph are indented. Newspapers frequently use hanging indents.

Paragraph and hanging indents are used primarily with blocks of copy. Copy blocks can be indented from the left, right, or both margins. Indents should be used consistently.

Setting indents with QuarkXPress

In QuarkXPress indents are set up using the **Formats** menu command under the **Style** menu. The options available in the **Paragraph formats** dialog box (right) allow you to create left, right, hanging, and left-and-right indents.

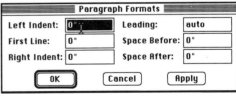

If you need to typeset spaces that are identical in size, be careful to use an unchanging space (like an em space). Do not use the space bar. Remember, in typography *word* spaces vary in width according to the justification needs of a line.

The most common widths are em, en, and thin spaces. An em is a square formed by the value of the point size. For example, a 9-point em space will be 9 points wide no matter what the face. An en space is half an em space, and a thin space is either $1/4$ or $1/5$ of an em. A figure space has the same width as the numerals 0–9 and the dollar sign, although an en space may be used instead of a figure space in some systems.

Ems, ens, and thins

On the Macintosh keyboard and in most desktop systems, typing **Option-Space** produces an en space, not an em space. To get an em you must type **Option-Space** twice.

| Indented one em (2 ens)
| Indented two ems (4 ens)
| Indented three ems (6 ens)
| Indented four ems (8 ens)

If you require fixed spaces of a certain number of points, remember that the em is as wide as the point size. If you need two picas of horizontal space, set 2 ems in 12-point (1 pica = 12 points).

| Two ems in 12-point type
| Two ems in 10-point type
| Two ems in 9-point type

Thus, if a designer specifies 6 picas, go to 12-point and key the **Option-Space** combination 12 times.

| Like this.

The em is also the maximum relative unit value, so, in a 100-unit system, the em is 100 units. The same is true for older 18- and 36- unit systems. Most phototypesetting systems use 18, 36, 72, and 108 units.

Although it sounds correct, the em is *not* related to the letter M. In some fonts it is possible that the letter M is one em wide, but this would be coincidental.

The em space is also a square with sides equal to the point size. For example, with 12-point type an em space is 12 points high by 12 points wide. The en space is half as wide as the em, and the thin space one-third or one-quarter of the width of the em.

Desktop Typography with QuarkXPress

**Creating thin spaces
with QuarkXPress**

 There is no thin space in the desktop world. However, you can create a thin space in QuarkXPress by using the **Horizontal Scale** command in the **Style** menu. Drag the cursor to select a space. Select the **Horizontal Scale** command and enter a value in the **Horiz scale** text field (the value can be as low as 10 percent). You can copy and paste these thin spaces repeatedly to create a space of the desired width.

Variations in the width of spaces occur when type is condensed or expanded. In these cases, although the letters remain the same height as the original point size, the widths of the fixed spaces vary according to the scaling values.

| Three ems at 100 percent width
| Three ems condensed to 80% of original width

Whether the em space is viewed as a square of the point size or not, the value is always equal to the maximum number of units. An increase in point size not only increases the size of the fixed spaces but also increases proportionately the size of the units. Therefore, units are relative. The larger the point size being used, the larger each of the units will be, but the *number* of units will not change. Always remember, an em has no value until you select the point size.

If you must indent a number of lines equally, set a tab position instead of keying multiple en spaces. It works much better and cuts keystroking time.

All typefaces, regardless of size, essentially align on an invisible horizontal reference line called a *baseline*.

HHabdgjklpqtyHH

This alignment is necessary so that a variety of styles and sizes can be mixed in the same line.

Horizontal alignment is based on the baseline.

Vertical alignment is based on the margins.

|MARGIN   MARGIN|

Desktop Typography with QuarkXPress

Machines can only align items according to preset reference points—thus, the need for human review for optical alignment.

Optical alignment involves the use of a visual "reference" point. For instance, when setting vertical lines of type, characters are not flushed left, they are centered.

Quotes set in the body typeface that are longer than five lines should be set apart from the rest of the body copy. There are several ways of doing this.

1. Set the quoted material one point size smaller than the body face. Leading should be no larger than two points more than the quoted material's size.

2. Indent two picas from both the left and right margins. Some typesetters and typographers indent two picas from the left only — with the right margin remaining the same as body copy.

3. Adding extra points of leading before and after the quoted material is a matter of style. Extra leading can be added for appearance, but never add as much as one complete line of white space.

4. Indented quotes do not begin and end with quotemarks. Setting the quote apart from the body copy eliminates the need for quotemarks, and you should make sure the typed material reflects this style. Single quotes appearing within the quoted section will become double quotemarks.

5. Paragraph indents in quoted matter should be one additional pica in width.

6. Significant omission of copy in a long quoted section (significant meaning whole paragraphs or sections) is sometimes shown by asterisks rather than by points of ellipsis. To set asterisks for this purpose, add 4 to 6 points of leading before the next line of copy, which will be 3 asterisks centered with two fixed spaces before and after the middle asterisk. Continue on the next line with the following line of copy. Asterisks showing omitted copy do not appear on the same typeset line as copy; points of ellipsis should be used in these instances.

Indenting quoted material

Chapter 7

Spacing

Spacing can be either horizontal or vertical or both:

- between letters
- between words
- between lines
- between text and heads
- between text and art

Word spacing

Spacing between printed words is largely a matter of the mechanics of composition. The operator puts a space after each word, and when the line is justified, the word spaces are expanded or condensed to accommodate the line of type on the specified line length. Spacing between words varies slightly from line to line in justified material, but all word spacing in a single line should be the same. Unequal word spaces in a line should be marked by the proofreader. A line with narrow spacing is called a *close* line, one with wide spacing an *open* line.

|Word word word word|
EM spaces — much too wide

|Word word word word word|
EN spaces—still too wide

|Word word word word word|
Word spaces set at 16—perfecto!

|Wordiwordiwordiwordiword|
Lowercase i

Close and open lines

Excessively wide word spacing detracts from readability, is unsightly, and should be avoided. Also, spaces on a number of successive open lines may produce the printing phenomenon known as a *river*—white ribbons that meander vertically down the page and distract the eye of the reader. For this reason, modern composition methods generally aim for close word spacing.

This is as example of an open line.

This is an example of a close line.

Desktop Typography with QuarkXPress

**Word spacing
with QuarkXPress**

 In QuarkXPress the values for the word spaces are set at the beginning of the job using the choices available in the **Preferences** menu command under the **Edit** menu. Click on **H&J** in the **Preferences** dialog box. The Hyphenation & Justification dialog box will appear. You can specify the following methods for justification expansion:

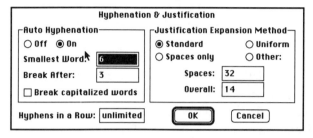

- **Standard.** More space is inserted between words than between characters. XPress automatically enters 16 for Spaces and 7 for Overall. This gives the best looking typography.
- **Uniform.** Excess space is divided as evenly as possible between characters. Automatically enters 0 for Spaces and 50 for Overall. Avoid this choice, since it can result in open lines.
- **Spaces only.** Excess space is only added between words. Automatically enters 50 for Spaces and 0 for Overall.
- **Other.** Lets you enter any values in Spaces and Overall.

The values for these four choices are entered in the appropriate dialog boxes:

- **Spaces** This refers to the maximum value of word spaces in a line. The range is 0–50 (en space width). Values between 16 and 20 are preferred.
- **Overall** This refers to the maximum space added between all character pairs, including character-to-word-space pairs. Letterspacing is an acknowledgment of your inability to control the typography. Set this value at zero and let the words fall where they will. For special cases, you can insert discretionary hyphens or you can override the standard hyphenation of a word with the **Hyphenation Exceptions** menu command in the **Utilities** menu.

Letterspacing is, very simply, the space between letters. Letterspacing values can be either positive and negative—you either add space or subtract space

Positive values for letterspacing should be avoided. All letters within words of a given typeface should be separated from each other by the same amount of space. Authors and editors should be aware, however, that some combinations of letters, particularly in the italic alphabet, give the illusion of more space between them.

Letterspacing

ABCabcdefGHIjklMNOpqrSTUvwxyz at -5
ABCabcdefGHIjklMNOpqrSTUvwxyz at -4
ABCabcdefGHIjklMNOpqrSTUvwxyz at -3
ABCabcdefGHIjklMNOpqrSTUvwxyz at -2
ABCabcdefGHIjklMNOpqrSTUvwxyz at -1
ABCabcdefGHIjklMNOpqrSTUvwxyz Normal
ABCabcdefGHIjklMNOpqrSTUvwxyz at +1
ABCabcdefGHIjklMNOpqrSTUvwxyz at +2
ABCabcdefGHIjklMNOpqrSTUvwxyz at +3
ABCabcdefGHIjklMNOpqrSTUvwxyz at +4
ABCabcdefGHIjklMNOpqrSTUvwxyz at +5

Examples of negative and positive letterspacing

Adding Letterspacing. Space is added between letters in the same increments for one or more of the following reasons:

Adjusting letterspaces

- Automatic letterspacing can be activated to ensure that word spaces do not become too wide during justification. By using this function you can preset a maximum width for word spaces.
- Selective letterspacing can be created for special character combinations (such as r and n, which might look like an m if spacing is too tight as in the example below).

r n   rn

- Letterspacing can be widened for aesthetic reasons, such as in all-capital titles or headings in which extra space is used as a design element.

Subtracting Letterspacing. Space between letters may also be compressed:

- Tight spacing (or white space reduction) is required for artistic reasons.
- Selective subtraction *(kerning)* is needed for certain character combinations.

The word "kern" can be used as a noun or a verb or even an adjective in the case of "kerned." Kerning reduces the space between characters and can cause characters to overlap; it is an "optical function." The space between certain letter combinations is reduced until it *looks right*.

Kerning is the use of negative letterspacing between certain character combinations to reduce the space between them. Characters in typesetting have specific width values and are actually positioned within an imaginary rectangle. Below, the right side wall of the W will touch the left side wall of the a, but because of the shape of these two letters, a gap will result:

Wa Wa Wa Wa Wa

Normal kern   **Minus 3**   **Minus 6**   **Minus 9**   **Minus 12**

In kerning, the space is reduced by "fooling" the printout device. We subtract a certain number of units from the width of the W's rectangle. The system then moves less units than would normally be required for the character's width; the subsequent letter "overlaps" to reduce the intercharacter space.

 QuarkXPress lets you specify the kerning and tracking values from the function under the **Style** menu. Use the **hyphen** when specifying negative values. If you have selected a group of characters, the **Tracking** dialog box is available. If the cursor is between two characters, the **Kerning** dialog box appears.

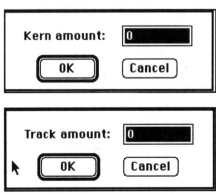

Kern amount: [0]   OK   Cancel

Track amount: [0]   OK   Cancel

Topographic kerning defines characters in terms of their *shape* as well as their width. Thus, a computer could *match* shapes on an almost infinite basis. In QuarkXPress, when you select **Auto Kerning** from the **Preferences** function under the **Edit** menu, the program uses the automatic tracking built into the fonts by the manufacturer. However, you may not be satisfied with the change to the appearance of the type, making manual kerning necessary. You can do manual kerning in $1/20$th of an em space increments by placing the insertion bar between the two characters you want to tighten and typing ⌘-**Shift-{** Add space by typing ⌘-**Shift-}** You can change the increments to $1/200$th of an em space by holding down the **Option** key with the aforementioned key combinations.

Some typesetting systems can kern more than 200 character pairs that you predefine automatically. However, after you have taken care of the 20 or so primary pairs, you are limited to a few hundred. If you add a few hundred more, you'll need even more for consistency. If you cannot kern *infinitely*, you may as well stay with the top 20—anything after that is a numbers game.

Here are the kern combinations that require corrective action:

Romano's Top-20 kerned pairs

1. Yo 2. We 3. To 4. Tr 5. Ta
6. Wo 7. Tu 8. Tw 9. Ya 10. Te
11. P. 12. Ty 13. Wa 14. yo 15. we
16. T. 17. Y. 18. TA 19. PA 20. WA

You can also kern letter pairs in QuarkXPress by placing the cursor between two characters and selecting the **Kern** menu command under the **Style** menu. When the **Kern** dialog box appears, you can specify a negative (use the **hyphen** as a minus sign) or positive (**no hyphen**) value. You will see the characters move together or apart after you click **OK.**

If you want to affect an entire block of copy, select it and go to the same place in the **Style** menu (only now it will say **Tracking**) and specify a negative or positive value in the **Tracking** dialog box.

Leading

The space between lines of type is called *leading* or *leads* (pronounced *ledding* and *leds*)because in hand and machine composition this space was created by inserting strips of lead between lines of type. To make more space between lines of text is to *lead it* or to *lead it out*. To *close up* lines—to create less space between them—is to *delete leads*.

Leading is measured in *points* and is always specified for each type size used. Where increased leading is necessary—before and after extracts, for example—the number of points is usually specified. When someone wants "more space" to indicate a new section in the text, the words *blank line* circled in the margin or in the space itself indicate how much space is to be inserted. A number sign space mark (#) is usually used to indicate extra space.

To determine the appropriate amount of leading requires consideration of a number of factors. The first of these, for text matter at any rate, is readability, and this largely depends on the type measurements. As type becomes larger, more leading is required to prevent the eye from being distracted by the lines above and below the one being read.

Also, the wider the line of type, the greater the leading needed, because in moving from the end of one line to the beginning of the next the eye takes a long jump. In closely set material the eye may easily jump to the wrong line.

Varying point size to determine overall length

Another factor to consider when choosing type size is economy of space. A relatively small type size and reduced leading allows more words per page, resulting in a thinner book and reduced costs for paper and mailing (weight). On the other hand, increasing point size and leading increases the overall size of a typeset piece.

Some simple rules for determining proper leading:

- Space lines as evenly as possible.
- The last line of a paragraph should not be less than one third the width of the line. An end line less than one third the line width is called is a widow.
- The last word of a paragraph should not be divided if possible, and a line should never be less than four characters long. A line less than four characters long that is carried to the next page is called an orphan.
- Division of the last word in a paragraph can be avoided by opening up or closing up the paragraph (enter appropriate letterspacing values). Transpose small words or short syllables of

hyphenated words at the ends of lines to the next line, thus putting an extra word or two on the next to the last line containing the one full word. If only a few units are needed to avoid dividing the last word, take one unit out between several words in the line to make room.

Typewriters and computer printers deal with fixed line spacing—usually six or eight lines to an inch.

Line spacing

```
Line 1      Line 1      Line 1
Line 2
Line 3      Line 2

            Line 3      Line 2
```

Single Spaced   Double Spaced Triple Spaced

Typography varies interline spacing according to:

- the type size
- the amount of extra spacing desired

Tiny amounts of space can be removed from or added between lines of type. You can stretch or compress a column vertically to fit a particular depth. This technique is known as *carding* and *feathering,* a carryover from the days of metal type. Thus, you can "lead out" text to fill more space by increasing the leading slightly. The amount of increase can be so small that it is not noticed as excessive leading.

Lines of type set solid (leading equals point size) can be difficult to read, so almost all lines need some leading. Some small x-height typefaces can be set without additional leading. Conversely, lines that have too much interline space can be difficult to read.

Since leading involves blank or white space, it not easy to visualize. However, think of the space between lines in terms of what they originally were: strips of metal.

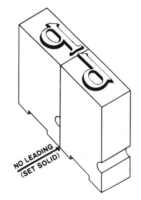

NO LEADING (SET SOLID)

_____

To give you an idea of leading, the line above this line is 1 point wide.

_____

The line above this line is 2 points wide.

_____

The line above this line is 4 points wide.

_____

The line above this line is 8 points wide.

Leading should be proportional to line length and point size—about 20 percent more than the point size. Some typographers say the leading of a block of text should be slightly larger than the optimum word space. In the days of hot metal type, very narrow spacing was called "carding" because strips of paper were used.

Minus leading

One of the capabilities that modern typesetting techniques makes available is called "minus leading." This means that the type can be set with leading that is less than the point size, 9-point type on 8.5-point leading, for example. Usually, this is done with type that is small or has short ascenders and descenders. It can also be done with material that is all caps—headlines, for example.

abcdefghABCDEFijklmnopGHIJKLMqrstuvwxyz___
abcdefghABCDEFijklmnopGHIJKLMqrstuvwxyz___
12-point type on 12-point leading

abcdefghABCDEFijklmnopGHIJKLMqrstuvwxyz___
abcdefghABCDEFijklmnopGHIJKLMqrstuvwxyz___
12-point type on 11-point leading

Small x-height typefaces and some small-on-body sans serif should have minimal or even minus leading.

To calculate the minimum amount of leading possible between two lines of type, especially when you are changing point sizes, take one third of the present point size and add it to two thirds of the point size to be used on the next line. If you do not have the proper leading, the lines could overlap one another.

The most important point to remember is that in typesetting all leading is measured from baseline to baseline.

abcdefghABCDEFijklmnopwxyz

abcdefghABCDEFijklmnopwxyz

abcdefghABCDEFijklmnopGHIJKLMqrstuvwxyz

abcdefghABCDEFijklmnopGHIJKLMqrstuvwxyz

abcdefghABCDEFijklmnopGHIJKLMqrstuvwxyz

abcdefghABCDEFijklmnopGHIJKLMqrstuvwxyz

abcdefghABCDEFijklmnopGHIJKLMqrstuvwxyz

abcdefghABCDEFijklmnopGHIJKLMqrstuvwxyz

The distance from baseline to baseline includes both the point size of the type and the incremental value of any leading that may be present.

Today, almost all type is leaded at least one point, even small x-height typefaces. Since most text is between 9-point and 12-point, it is unusual to see more than three points of leading.

In the following sample paragraphs, the leading ranges from minus 1 point to plus 3 points. Which paragraph do you think is the most legible? Look carefully.

Leading examples

The space between lines is called leading (pronounced ledding). These leads varied in thickness so that they could be inserted after type was set to space the line out according to the desires of the designer, the standards of the typographer, and the needs of the job.
10 on 9

The space between lines is called leading (pronounced ledding). These leads varied in thickness so that they could be inserted after type was set to space the line out according to the desires of the designer, the standards of the typographer, and the needs of the job.
10 on 10

The space between lines is called leading (pronounced ledding). These leads varied in thickness so that they could be inserted after type was set to space the line out according to the desires of the designer, the standards of the typographer, and the needs of the job.
10 on automatic

The space between lines is called leading (pronounced ledding). These leads varied in thickness so that they could be inserted after type was set to space the line out according to the desires of the designer, the standards of the typographer, and the needs of the job.
10 on 11

The space between lines is called leading (pronounced led-ding). These leads varied in thickness so that they could be inserted after type was set to space the line out according to the desires of the designer, the standards of the typographer, and the needs of the job.

10 on 12

The space between lines is called leading (pronounced led-ding). These leads varied in thickness so that they could be inserted after type was set to space the line out according to the desires of the designer, the standards of the typographer, and the needs of the job.

10 on 13

The paragraphs leaded one and two points more than the 10-point type are easiest on the eyes.

Setting leading in QuarkXPress

 There are three methods for specifying leading in QuarkXPress. You can set leading with a precision of 0.001 point.

1. Leading can be specified using the **Preferences** command in the **Edit** menu. The auto default (20%) setting in the Preferences dialog box means that leading will be equal to the point size of the type plus 20 percent. You may enter other values in the Leading text field, but for body text, you will probably want to stay around the 100–120 percent value.

This feature can be useful if you must change point sizes to meet a design requirement or to make text fit in a specified number of pages. However, many of us who lived through the days of hot metal and phototypesetting are accustomed to numeric values for leading; we were not trained to figure with percentages.

Leading by percentages

You can use a calculator to determine leading percentages. Divide the leading value you want (12, for example) by the point size (10 in this case) and hit the **Percent** key (20%). Or you can develop a quick reference chart like the one below until you develop an awareness of various values:

Point Size	Percent	Lead Value
6	10%	.6 point
6	16.6%	1 point
6	20%	1.2 point
7	10%	.7 point

7	14.3%	1 point
7	20%	1.4 point
8	10%	.8 point
8	12.5%	1 point
8	20%	1.6 point
9	10%	.9 point
9	11.1%	1 point
9	20%	1.8 point
10	10%	1 point
10	20%	2 points
11	10%	1.1 point
11	9.1%	1 point
11	20%	2.2 points
12	10%	1.2 point
12	8.3%	1 point
12	20%	2.4 points

This chart will help you get a better feel for specifying leading as a percentage rather than as a specific value.

 2. QuarkXPress, allows you to set leading values using the **Formats** menu command under the **Style** menu. Enter the numeric value you want in the Leading text field in the Paragraph Formats dialog box.

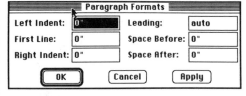

Additional ways of setting leading values with QuarkXPress

3. You can also increase or reduce the leading of a range of selected text in 1 point increments. The keyboard combination **Shift-Option-⌘ -;** decreases the leading of the selected text. **Shift-Option-⌘ -'** increases the leading. (This keyboard function will only work if "auto" is *not* entered in the Leading text field in the Paragraph formats dialog box—pictured above).

For those of you who would like some specific guidance, the following list contains suggestions for leading values (in points):

Romano's Rules for Leading

Size	Minimum	Optimum	Maximum
6	Solid	1	1
7	Solid	1	1.5
8	Solid	1.5	2

8	Solid	1.5	2
9	Solid	2	2.5
10	solid	2	2.5
11	−1	2	3
12	−1	2.5	3.5
14	−1	2.5	4

If you need to calculate how many lines there would be in one inch at particular leading values, use the following chart:

Size	Lines to Inch
6	12
7	10.285
8	9
9	8
10	7.2
11	6.545
12	6
14	5.143
18	4
24	3
36	2
48	1.5
72	1

Leading in headlines

One of the areas in which leading is critical is the setting of headings:

This heading is set
with 2 points
leading
(24 on 26)

This heading is set with no leading (24 on 24)

This heading is set with minus leading (24 on 23)

The most important consideration concerns those areas where ascenders and descenders meet. Too often typesetters have little control over how the copy falls. Consequently, unsightly problems may arise.

To avoid overlapping ascenders and descenders in headlines, some people use ALL CAP heads. Don't give in to the dark side of the the ALL CAP Force: make type work for you. Some very creative headline approaches have been developed to get around copy that has ascenders and descenders falling in the worst possible places.

The most important aspect of spacing is consistency. The following is a checklist:

Consistency

- Is the text leading the same for all copy blocks?
- Is the spacing before and after heads and subheads the same?
- Are the left and right margins consistent?
- Is the spacing around folios consistent?
- Is the spacing around running heads and feet consistent?
- Is the spacing between illustrations and text the same?
- Is the spacing between illustrations and captions the same?
- Are all paragraph indents the same?

Chapter 8

Characters

The evolution of alphabetic characters (or written communication, if you like) was not an organized progression. Three "forces" — Phoenician, Greek, and Roman — shaped our alphabet, with the Roman influence being the most important. More than anything else, the development of the alphabet was influenced by national habits, and only the eventual spread of printing brought "standardization."

The evolution of the alphabet

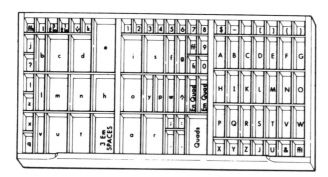

Printer's single tray type case

As the demand for written material increased, scribes tended to write faster and faster. Consequently, they developed "short cuts" to create serifs and terminal strokes with *fluid* motions of the pen instead of separate strokes.

Speed leads to change

The trend toward *cursive* writing resulted in speed (which led to an increase in productivity) and—as byproducts—symmetry, beauty, and simplicity. The need to write rapidly brought us the *minuscule*.

The minuscule

For years, the *uncial* (Latin *uncus*, crooked) was a capital letter that rounded the straight lines. The uncial was a *majuscule* and was modified over time to become the *half uncial*, the manuscript style of the 8th century.

Lowercase letters also evolved from the scribe's need to write faster. Two handwriting styles — the *formal* hand of the church and royalty and the *informal* hand of administrators and scholars — developed over the centuries. The Caroline minuscule is the direct ancestor of our lowercase.

The appearance of lowercase letters

The term lowercase is derived from the layout of the printer's type case, which had the capital letters in the upper part and the small letters in the lower part. Upper case refers to capital letters and mixed case means the first letter of each word is capitalized.

Lowercase = Unshift
Upper case = Shift

None of this evolution was deliberate or organized. Within each geographic area eccentricities developed. For instance, there were several Roman hands: Square Capitals, Rustic Capitals, Everyday Hand, and Roman Cursive. The Uncials evolved from the Rustic Capitals and the Everyday Hand; the Half Uncials came more from the Cursive Hand. And it was Charlemagne who decreed that all book writing throughout his kingdom — which in A.D. 800 was the Holy Roman Empire — was to be done in a standard hand: the Caroline Minuscule, as it is called today.

Standardization

Thus, in the 1500s and 1600s as printing spread throughout Europe, it became possible to adapt national hands to this "standard." As a result, many of the stylistic characteristics that had been eliminated in the rush for faster handwriting were resurrected. The alphabet was just about complete.

In 1585, Louis Elzevir was the first to use "v" and "j" as consonants and "i" and "u" as vowels. These letters were universally adopted in 1822. Since type cases did not have provision for the new "j" and "u," they were added to the end of the alphabet after the "z."

Lowercase letters are easier to read because their shapes are distinct, whereas caps create a monotonous shape in a line.

Lowercase gives us easy-to-recognize word shapes

The letters A through Z and (usually) the ampersand represent the alphabet as we know it. All-cap words and acronyms in text look best as SMALL CAPS rather than ALL CAPS. In heads, all-capped words as well as all-cap groups of words are usually set as caps with minimum word spacing and are occasionally letterspaced slightly.

Specifiying characters with QuarkXPress

 Any selected character or group of characters can be specified in terms of typographic and stylistic presentation with QuarkXPress:

Select the **Character** menu command under the **Style** menu to bring up the Character Specifications dialog box. In this dialog box you can specify Font, Size, and Style (plain, bold, italic, etc.; see illustration on next page) for the selected text. You can also specify Shade, Color, Track amount, Horizontal scale.

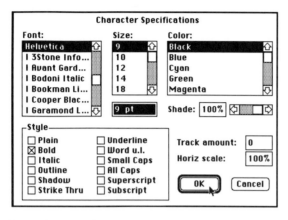

Quark XPress' Character Specification dialog box

Because many people are accustomed to thinking of character size in terms of points, you may want to relate point size to cap height. Caps range from approximately 66 percent to not more than 83 percent of body size.

Small caps are capital letters designed to match the x-height of a particular typeface and size:

HXHxABCDHXH

24-point Times caps alongside 18-point Times caps

HXHxABCDHXH

24-point Times caps alongside small caps horizontally scaled at 120 percent

Since many fonts currently do not have small caps, they are "manufactured" by reducing the point size of the type two sizes, setting capital letters, and then returning to the original size. This method is not accurate because small caps are supposed be 80 percent as high as regular caps. Artificially produced small caps are not true small caps; they may be lighter than the caps and look out of place. "True-cut" small caps are usually equal to the normal cap width; reduced caps are slightly narrower. That's

Small caps

Desktop Typography with QuarkXPress

because they were on the same hot metal matrix as the cap character and thus had to have the same width as the wider character. Digitized typesetting devices have an advantage in being able to reduce size in smaller increments and to electronically expand character to form small caps.

 To create small caps in QuarkXPress, select the text you want to modify. Type ⌘-**Shift-H** to change the selected text to small caps. You can also create small caps using the **Character** menu command under the **Style** menu.

Words in text that are specified as all caps may look better (in terms of the typographic color of the page) in small caps. This is also true of lining figures — they look best slightly smaller. Old Style figures look best with small caps.

January 8, 1926
JANUARY 8, 1926

Small caps should be used for abbreviations of awards, decorations, honors, titles, etc. following a person's name. The use of full cap initial letters with small caps is not advised. All small caps is preferred.

Use all caps or small caps for the following:

- for the word WHEREAS in resolutions
- for the word NOTE introducing an explanatory paragraph that cannot be used as a footnote
- for the words SECTION and ARTICLE in reference to part of a document by number
- for the speaker in a dialogue or play
- for ascription to author of a direct, independent quotation
- for words ordinarily in italics that appear in all-cap-and-small-cap or in an all-small-cap line
- for the abbreviations A.M. and P.M. (*ante* and *post meridiem*) and B.C. and A.D. ("Before Christ" and *anno Domini*). These should be set without a space between letters.

Headlines

Editors derived two "standard" conventions for capitalizing headlines: *upstyle* and *downstyle*. Upstyle heads follow standard capitalization rules. Use caps for all words except conjunctions, articles, and prepositions of three or fewer letters. Capitalize the words Between, With, Over, Down, Around, Under, but lower-case on, at, the, a, etc., unless the word is emphasized.

Some publications capitalize "to" when it's part of an infinitive. Examples: Capitalize To in *To Run*, *To Shoot*, but lowercase to when used as a preposition, such as in "to Office" and "to China." The object is consistency. Decide on your style and stick to it; don't capitalize "to" if it is used as a preposition.

In downstyle headlines, the first word and all proper nouns are capitalized. Which style should you choose, upstyle or down-style? Downstyle.

A Cap & Lowercase Headline

A downstyle headline

A SMALL CAP HEADLINE

Caps & Small Caps Headline

ALL SMALL CAPS HEADLINE

Abbreviations: Follow standard abbreviation rules in headlines, but watch out for:

Abbreviations

- Less well known abbreviations and acronyms. We all know FBI, CIA and YMCA, but less familiar acronyms should be spelled out..
- Regional uses. IRT means trains in New York City.
- Months. Abbreviate the long months and spell out short ones, such as June and July.
- Days of the week. Standard rules say to spell them out.
- Large numbers. Some styles allow abbreviating million and billion when they concern money amounts.

For example:

Board OK's $6M. expansion.

- Note the period after the M. (Note also the apostrophe in OK's. It's optional.)

Accents

Accents: Originally, the term "accent" meant "accented characters" — that is, the combination of a character *and* its appropriate accent, such as the ñ (pronounced *"ny"*) in Spanish or the ç, (pronounced *"s"*) in French. The accents in these examples, the tilde and the cedilla, combine with the character to form a specialized character. These characters are used primarily for pronunciation purposes and foreign language words.

Today, most accented characters do not exist as a single unit Instead, they are formed by combining standard characters and placing related accents above, below, or through the character. The accents most often used are:

Acute	é á í
Angstrom	å Å
Cedilla	ç Ç
Circumflex	ô û
Dieresis (also called Umlaut)	ö ï ë
Grave	è à ò
Tilde	ñ Ñ

Note that when the accent is specified for the lowercase i, the dot disappears.

The accent is stored as a separate character in most cases, with zero width (no escapement value). Thus, it "floats" above or below a character position. Accents used in this manner are designed for the weight, style, and height (cap and lowercase) of a typeface.

There are two ways of creating accented characters. Some fonts are manufactured with special accented characters built in. However, in many desktop typography situations, accents are created using the **Option** key. For example, type **Option-n** (the cursor doesn't move) followed by **n** to create ñ. In these two-key combinations, the first (Option) character is the accent, the second character is a letter. In these cases, the output device selects the accent, positions it with no escapement, then positions the character, which escapes normally.

Some typefaces have multiple versions of the same letter in the font to allow a greater variety of letter combinations. Specimen showings normally show all character variants with an identifying number of specification purposes.

Alternative characters

Multiple versions of the same character are available to allow more creativity in headline setting. The key to their use is *restraint*—use as few as possible. Most alternate characters are "swash" versions that over- and under-hang adjacent characters.

Swash: A swash-type character is one designed with a "flourish" at the beginning or end. "Bookman" was one of the first typefaces to have alternate characters.

Swash

Ampersand: The ampersand (&) was originally a ligature (*et*, Latin for *and*) and did double duty as part of the alphabet. It was placed at the end, as "*et per se, and*" (that is, et by itself, and) which became corrupted to "and per se and." In some ampersand designs, the e and t are distinguishable. A small cap ampersand often works better than the regular cap version, especially when used with lowercase letters. Ampersands are used primarily in titles and company names.

Ampersand

Caps & Lowercase (cap &)
Caps & Lowercase (small cap &)

Arrows: These are available in many pi fonts. Arrows come in open and closed versions, pointing in most directions (left, right, up, and down), and combinations. The following are some arrows from the Zapf Dingbats font:

Arrows

Desktop Typography with QuarkXPress

Dashes

Dashes: Ranging from the smallest to the largest, here are the dashes that are used in typography:

- Hyphen
– En Dash
— Em Dash

Hyphens

The hyphen is used for breaking words between syllables at the end of lines to create even spacing in justified type and for compound or connected words *(mother-in-law)*.

The meaning of a hyphen is to *connect*.

- *Always* use a hyphen when breaking a word at the end of a line of type.
- *Always* use a hyphen when connecting two or more words to create a compound phrase, such as mind-building exercises, non-hyphenated justification.
- *Never* use any space before a hyphen.
- Use space after a hyphen *only* in such cases: "the long- and short-run," "two- and three-year olds."
- The first sign of typographic inexperience is the use of a hyphen when a dash is correct.

En dash

The en dash is used in place of the words the "to" and "through," such as "Pages 1–9" or "January 13–19." It also connects two nouns of equal weight, such as "East–West" alliance. If you do not have an en dash, kern two hyphens together. The en dash should always be closed (no space on either side).

– En Dash
-- Two hyphens
– Two hyphens kerned
— Em Dash

The en dash is one-half the length of an em dash and is longer than a hyphen (in typing, a hyphen is used for an en dash, two hyphens for an em dash; in preparing the manuscript, the editor will then indicate where en dashes are to be set). The principal use of the en dash is to indicate continuing, or inclusive, numbers—dates, time, or reference numbers.

The en dash is also used in place of a hyphen in a compound adjective in which one element consists of two words or a hyphenated word:

>   New York–London flight
>   post–Civil War period
>   quasi-public–quasi-judicial body
>   *but:* non-English-speaking countries.

The en dash is a slightly small em dash and is used in places where an em dash would look too wide for the typeface in use. Usually, you cannot modify the width of the dash, so forget it.

The em dash (and 3/4 em if you have it) is used to indicate missing material such as "Dr.—was the murderer" and for parenthetical remarks to show a break in thought or special emphasis, such as "Hello—he thought at the time—." Em dashes are also used to replace a colon. For example, "Here's the list—".

Em dash

Em dashes may be open, with a word space on both sides, or closed, with no space. The open style allows for more alternatives for end-of-line breaks, although some newer systems will break at an Em dash if it occurs at the end of a line.

>   Open — Open
>   Closed—Closed

You should try to avoid carrying dashes over to the beginning of the following line.

When a dash must occur at the end of a justified line, it is correct to place the dash either at the end of that line or at the beginning of the next line. (This is not true of a hyphen; it may occur only at the end of a line.)

In *some* cases, either a fixed space or a space bar is used before and after a dash. However, this should be done only if specified. Using space bars around a dash in justified copy may cause awkward gaps because the sizes of these spaces will vary. This is why closed dashes are more common.

Never use two dashes together.

The rule line (often, but not always, aligning at the baseline) is used for horizontal ruling and underlining.

Points of Ellipsis

Points of Ellipsis: Points of ellipsis are better known as the "three periods" that indicate that something is missing (omission) or that conversation has stopped (interruption). If a sentence is complete, the period is set close, followed by the three points.

Points of ellipsis show that an author is purposely leaving out a word or words when quoting from someone else. They can also be used to express a pause or break in thought.

The following examples show how to use points of ellipsis:

> He explained, "Now that were are here...we will begin."
> "To be...or not to be...that is the question."

When copy is left out in the middle of a sentence, use three periods, but:

. . . Spaced with word spaces
. . . Spaced with en spaces
... Spaced using **Option ;** on the Macintosh keyboard

The last version is best. The space should be fixed, not variable (as it would be with word spaces) and about half the size of an en space.

Use four periods (use the point of ellipsis and add another period instead of the word, space bar) when copy is left out at the end of a sentence (the fourth period acts as the period of the sentence). Only if someone demands it should you use more periods. The copy may be given to you that way, but most people prefer that you typeset correctly. You may, however, run across copy that has been specified to create an "effect."

"The end is near....or, at least, close."

The problem with these darned dots is that they may fall at the end of a line, and then several things can happen.

- If you spaced them with fixed spaces, the program may see them as one unit and not break them, thus forcing a tight line or necessitating a badly spaced one.

- If you used word spaces between the periods, it will result in erratic spacing—too wide or too close—based on the justification requirements of the line. The word spaces will help if they fall at the end of the line.

- Insert a word space between the periods and the preceding word if you feel there will be a problem.

- Or, you can use "kerned word spaces" between the periods.

References refer to marginal, parenthetical, or reference material relating to the main body of text. Footnotes are references marked with certain symbols, letters, or numbers, most often in superior form, and are positioned at the bottom of the page.

References

A footnote must begin on the same page as its "reference call" but may be carried over to the bottom of successive pages or to the end of a section, chapter, or article. A short rule or additional space separates the footnote from the text. A footnote may also be placed at the end of its associated text. When done in this manner, they may also be called "references."

Footnotes are most often 7-point or 8-point. By law, footnotes in financial forms, annual reports, prospectuses, and other SEC documents may be no smaller than the text size, which is 10-point.

The sequence of footnote reference marks is:

Reference marks

Asterisk
Single Dagger
Double Dagger
Paragraph Symbol
Section Mark
Double Vertical Rule

And if you still need more, double up by using double asterisks, double (single) daggers, double double daggers, etc. Most foot-notes are referenced by superior numerals. Occasionally, in publications with only a handful of footnotes, the asterisk is used.

Footnote numbers should *follow* punctuation marks (except a dash).Whenever possible a footnote number should be placed at the end of a sentence, or at least at the end of a clause. Numbers set between subject and verb or between other related words in a sentence are distracting to the reader.

The proper placement of a footnote:

...said the coroner.[5]

Footnote numbers

The footnote number *follows* a quotation, whether the quotation is short and run into the text or long and set off from the text in reduced type. The number should not be inserted after the author's name or after matter preceding the quotation.

Placing footnote numbers at the end of, or within, a line of display type is discouraged. A footnote applicable to an entire chapter or article should be unnumbered and should appear on the first page of the chapter, before any numbered notes. A reference number that appears at the end of a subhead should be moved to an appropriate spot in the text.

Footnotes should be numbered consecutively, beginning with 1, throughout a chapter of a book or an article in a journal. Although in large scholarly books this sometimes results in three-digit numbers (undesirable particularly from a book designer's point of view), it is far more practical than the old-fashioned system of beginning with 1 on each page.

[5]**Ibid.**
[6]**Ibid.**

The old way can lead to confusion because manuscript pages and printed pages are rarely the same length. Consequently, the footnotes that appear together on a manuscript page may not be together on the printed page. This method requires that all footnote numbers and references to them must be checked, and often they must be reset in page proofs, a costly process and one subject to error. Also any cross-references to notes numbered by page rather than by chapter must include page numbers as well; "see note 3" is meaningless when a chapter contains more than one note 3.

Figures

The figures 0 through 9 come in two versions:

Old Style or Old Face (or Non-aligning)	1234567890
Lining (or Modern)	1234567890

In text, numbers under 10 should be spelled out unless they relate to specific references. Always spell out a number at the beginning of a sentence.

All figures must be the same width to allow vertical alignment when used in tabs or listings; this does not apply to dates.

Follow usual style rules for numbers. Use Arabic numbers (0123456789) for ages, addresses, temperatures, distances, scores, dimensions, money amounts, etc.

Use of numerals

Traditional text style calls for zero through nine to be spelled out and numbers 10 and up to appear as figures. When possible, follow the same style rules in headlines, although sometimes digits make more sense.

Numbers are not always repeated in type as they are written in the manuscript. Figures should be avoided as much as possible for all numbers except dates. This is easier said than done.

Be careful about old typing habits

Watch your old typing habits. The lowercase letter l (el) and the numeral 1 are different and should be typed as such. Similarly, the capital letter O and the digit 0 are not the same character.

1 l	1 l	1 l	1 l
o 0	o 0	o 0	o 0
Times	**Courier**	**Helvetica**	**Palatino**

There are no rigid rules for determining when and where to substitute figures for words. When great precision of statement is desired, as is customary in legal documents and in many other kinds of formal writing, figures and abbreviations should never be used if there is ample of space for words. Words are preferred for stating whole numbers in simple sentences:

> The basket held twenty apples.
> The engine has one hundred horsepower.
> The steamer's capacity is six thousand tons.

In most instances, words should be used for numbers of infrequent recurrence. Even when the numbers are large but not too frequent, words are preferred if space permits:

> The regiment consists of one hundred and forty-eight men.
> The returns showed twenty-nine killed, forty-four wounded, and twenty-six missing.

In ordinary description the expression of numbers by hundreds is preferred to that by thousands: twenty-eight hundred and sixty is a more approved phrase than two thousand eight hundred and sixty. In legal documents the opposite method prevails: dates appear by thousands; measurements, numeric values, and fractions in every form are spelled out.

More use of numerals

When space is limited and complex numbers appear often, words are a hindrance and are of no benefit to the reader. The information will be more quickly and easily discerned by figures. Clarity is the primary concern. Make the information as clear as possible to the reader.

It is not correct to use numbers in one chapter or paragraph and not in another. Uniformity of style should be maintained throughout a publication. It is better to cause slight offense by being overly precise than to cause even greater offense and confusion by varying the style among different paragraphs.

Words are always preferred for numbers, including the following examples.

> This indenture, made the twenty-seventh day of June, in the year of our Lord one thousand nine hundred and ninety-seven.

Words should also be used in all legal papers for the statement of moneys paid, as well as for the measurements of land and the expression of values. Using figures in instances such as these can easily lead to errors and misinterpretation. For this reason, statements of numbers plainly intended to have special distinction should be in words, even when they appear as arabic figures in ordinary writings. Even in compact writing the use of spelled-out words instead of figures is sometimes obligatory.

When a sentence begins with a number, words must be used, even if figures are used in other parts of the same sentence.

When any paragraph consists largely of numbers that specify quantities, weights, or measurements, these should be in words and the rates in figures. Dollar amounts should be expressed in numerals unless they are part of a legal contract (in which case you should use both forms). Of course, partial numbers should be in numeral form. Let common sense dictate your use of figures.

Seventy yards of calico, at $5^1/_2$ cents per yard.

Forty-five bushels of oats, at $37^1/_2$ cents per bushel.

Seventeen acres of land, at $12^3/_4$ per acre.

Part number 2345 is $45.16.

The price is $34.12.

When numerical statements like the ones above are repeated frequently, the restricted use of figures for rates or values makes a proper distinction between quantities and rates and helps the reader to a better understanding of the subject matter.

Arabic figures should be used to express degrees of heat (as in temperature 71F°) and specifications of gravity (as in Lead is 11.352), but words are better for degrees of inclination (as in "an angle of forty-five degrees").

Also use arabic figures for records of votes (as in 20 yeas to 41 nays) and when describing a competitor's time in a race (as in one mile in 2 minutes 23 seconds).

Numerals used as qualifiers are neater when expressed in words (as in two-foot rule and ten-story building); but when a noun is frequently repeated on the same page with different qualifiers, figures make the subject matter more understandable (as in 6-point, 24-point, and 60-point type). However, combining figures and words to create a compound word is not recommended.

In ordinary writing, dates should be expressed in arabic figures, but when they appear in legal documents words should be used. When the numerical day of the month precedes the month, it should appear with the appropriate characters, as in 10th April and 22nd April. When the number of the day follows the month, the *th* or *nd* is not required; as in April 10 and April 22. When the day of the month is specified in a document, it should be written out in full, as in "the tenth day of April" and "the twenty-second day of April."

Dates should be expressed uniformly in a publication. It is improper to have April 17, 1962, on one page, and 23d August, 1764, on another. The use of 2d and 3d, common in Great Britain, is not recommended; 2nd and 3rd are more acceptable abbreviations. If you use either form, use it consistently.

In formal writing a statement of time should be made using words. Phrases like two o'clock, half-past three, or ten minutes to four are better expressed by words than by 2 o'clock, 3:30 p.m., or 3.50.

Hours are occasionally separated from minutes by a period, as in 11.30. These days, it is more common to use the colon, as in 4:00 a.m. The forms o'clk and o'cl'k are archaic.

Figures are often used for time when followed by the abbreviations a.m. and p.m. When a.m. and p.m. are not in the copy, for example "at seven o'clock in the morning" and "at twelve o'clock noon," words should be used instead of figures.

In ordinary description, but not in a legal document, the expression of money in complex or broken amounts, $21.76, for example, should be expressed with figures. Even amounts of money, like five dollars and three shillings, may be in words, but not if figures are used in the same paragraph for other amounts. In ordinary composition, whole numbers with vulgar fractions often necessitate the use of figures.

Analysis showed $13\frac{1}{2}$ grains of soda to the pint.
John has $76.21, and James has $50.67.

An isolated "vulgar" fraction (as DeVinne called them) should be expressed in words. For example, 1/8th and 1/32nd are more readable when expressed as one eighth and one thirty-second. Should you use the em version of the phony fraction? If you have to use any, go for the phony.

The hyphen is not needed when expressing simple fractions, such as "one eighth. " But a hyphen is required when the fraction is used as a qualifier, as in "a one-eighth share."

In compounded fractions, such as "eight thirty-seconds," a hyphen is required for the compounded numeral to show the closer relation of the two numbers to each other. Another example is "forty-seven ninety-sixths."

When figures of very large amounts, such as 23,762 and 5,368,872, occur frequently, the thousands should be separated by a comma. It is not necessary to use a comma for numbers of only four figures, like 5962, nor should a comma be inserted between figures that express dates, like 1961.

Figures in a descriptive text are not visually pleasing, but they are necessary when the amounts are large and occur frequently. To express the figures in the preceding paragraph in words would require additional space and would not be easier for the reader to understand. In the texts of formal documents, however, words are preferred to figures, not only for their greater precision, but for their neater appearance.

Because figures are ascending letters, occupying two thirds of the height of the body, bunching them in a paragraph spots the page and produces the effect of the overbold display of many capital letters. But often neatness must be subordinated to clarity. Figures are more quickly read, are more compact, and are indispensable for tabular work.

The numerical names of city streets are best presented in words when the words are not repeated too frequently in the same sentence or paragraph. For example, First Street is better than 1st Street. One-hundred-and-sixty-first Street is a somewhat awkward term, but it should follow the aforementioned rule and should be uniform with other numerical words in the document.

The use of roman numerals is acceptable for expressing dates on title pages and in chapter headings. The most commonly used roman numerals are made from combinations of the seven capitals, I, V, X, L, C, D, and M:

Roman numerals

1	I	12	XII	30	XXX	500	D
2	II	13	XIII	40	XL	600	DC
3	III	14	XIV	50	L	700	DCC
4	IV	15	XV	60	LX	800	DCCC
5	V	16	XVI	70	LXX	900	CM
6	VI	17	XVII	80	LXXX	1000	M
7	VII	18	XVIII	90	XC	2000	MM
8	VIII	19	XIX	100	C	3000	MMM
9	IX	20	XX	200	CC		
10	X	21	XXI	300	CCC		
11	XI	22	XXII	400	CD		

When letters that represent numbers of low value follow a letter of high value, the low-value letters are added to the high value. For example, XIII stands for 13. When letters of low value precede a letter of high value, the preceding letters are subtracted from the letter of higher value that follows: MCM=1900.

Roman numerals had to be used by the first printers because they had no Arabic figures. Arabic figures were first used in 1471 by Ther Hoernen, but they did not obtain general acceptance until many years later. They were irregular in form and made bad mates for the roman capital letters.

These unsymmetrical Arabic characters were improved, but slowly, still remaining objectionably ostentatious at the close of the 18th century. The figures 1, 2, and 0 were made small and low, and all other figures were put above or below the line. For tabular work all the figures were cast upon an en body size. This made them look too small when they were used in a line of capitals.

Someday the metric system may negate all the variety, but the following examples are the forms of fractions:

Em Fractions: This is the most common form, with each fraction on the em width, with a diagonal stroke. Most font layouts include the 1/4, 1/2, and 3/4 characters. Some fonts do not have any fractions.

$$1^2/_3$$

The relationship of the whole number to numerator/denominator:

- Numerator and denominator are 60 percent of the whole number's point size and 70 percent of its width
- Denominator and whole number align at baseline
- Numerator aligns at top of whole number
- Fraction bar is set to whole number's point size
- Numerator is raised above baseline; bottom aligns with 40 percent of whole number's height

Desktop Typography with QuarkXPress

 Here is a quick method of making fractions with QuarkXPress (using 12-point as example):

1. Type **12/3** with no spaces
2. Select the numerator; use the **Type Style** menu command under the **Style** menu to change it to a superscript; use the **Size** menu command (also under the Style menu) to reduce it to 9 points
3. Change the denominator to 9-point
4. Result: 1²/₃

En Fractions: These are, of course, set on the en width and have a horizontal stroke. They are used when a vast number of odd fractions — 16ths, 32nds, etc. are required. en fractions are also called "Stack Fractions."

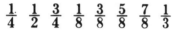

En fractions

Piece Fractions: These are created using en- and em -sized characters in only the denominators. The fractions are created using special numerals, such as the superiors, in combination with the denominator to form the full fraction.

Phony Fractions: These fractions are created when no font fractions are available by using the regular numerals separated by a slash. Make sure you use a hyphen to make 1 1/4 look like 1-1/4.

Decimal Fractions: For example, 1/4 = .25 and so on. Of course, you can spell the fraction out: 1/4 = one quarter.

Greek: Greek characters are used mainly in math but often appear in other instances (see chart of Greek characters on following page). Remember, the Greek alphabet has an upper case and a lower case.

The example below shows the Greek characters as they are accessed in English alphabetical order:

αβχδεφγηιφκλμνοπθρστυϖωξψζ
ΑΒΧΔΕΦΓΗΙϑΚΛΜΝΟΠΘΡΣΤΥςΩΞΨΖ

Desktop Typography with QuarkXPress

Leaders

Leaders are essentially dots or dashes that "lead" (pronounced *leed,* not *led*) the eye from one side of a line to the other. In hot metal, leaders were unique characters, with one leader dot centered on an en width or two leader dots set on an em width. The dots come in varying weights, ranging from fine, light dots to heavy, bold dots.

The hot metal linecaster provided various styles of leaders to meet different publishing and printing conditions. They varied primarily in weight of dot or stroke, in dots or strokes to the em, and in casting, in depth of punching.

Regular leaders vary in weight of dot or stroke to match the face and point size with which they are used. They are supplied in dot or hyphen style in two, four or six dots or strokes to the em.

Upper Case	Lower Case	Description
A	α	alpha
B	β	beta
X	χ	chi
Δ	δ	delta
E	ε	epsilon
H	η	eta
Γ	γ	gamma
I	ι	iota
K	κ	kappa
Λ	λ	lambda
M	μ	mu
N	ν	nu
Ω	ω	omega
O	ο	omicron
Φ	φ	phi
Π	π	pi
Ψ	ψ	psi
P	ρ	rho
Σ	σ ς	sigma
T	τ	tau
Θ	θ	theta
Υ	υ	upsilon
Ξ	ξ	xi
Z	ζ	zeta

The Greek alphabet

Today, the period is used most often as the leader dot. However, simple periods are not always the best solution. For instance, you might create better looking leaders by using periods of a smaller point size than the text.

Name..Address
Same size leader (12 point)

Name..Address
Smaller size leader (6 point)

Desktop Typography with QuarkXPress

Leaders should align vertically as well as horizontally. This is usually done automatically by the program. One of the problems with leaders is related to the mathematics of dividing their width into the line length. A 9-point leader, for instance, would divide into a 20 pica line (240 points) 26.66 times. The blank space that results must be placed somewhere in order to align copy at the margins, and some systems may not put the space where it looks best.

Here are some options:

1. Go to a lower point size for the period.

....
6 point

....
8 point

....
9 point

2. Key a word space at the beginning or end of the line, as a place for the excess space to go.

| .... |
With word space

|...........................|
Without word space

3. Use tracking to reduce the space between periods.

|...........................|
Normal tracking

|...........................|
Minus 2 tracking

4. Condense the width of the period.

|...........................|
Normal scaling
|...........................|
At 90 percent horizontal scaling

You can create leaders (using any character you wish as the leader) with QuarkXPress using the **Tabs** menu command under the **Style** menu. Set the kind of tab you want (left, right, centered, or decimal); in the Fill Character text field, enter the character you want as the leader.

Creating leaders

**Creating leaders
with QuarkXPress**

Here is the standard character chart:

Key Cap	Character	Shift Character	Option Character	Option Shift Character	Key Cap	Character	Shift Character	Option Character	Option Shift Character
A	a	A	å	Å	Y	y	Y	¥	À
B	b	B	∫	ı	Z	z	Z	Ω	Û
C	c	C	ç	Ç	1	1	!	¡	⁄
D	d	D	∂	Î	2	2	@	™	¤
E	e	E	´	‰	3	3	#	£	‹
F	f	F	ƒ	Ï	4	4	$	¢	›
G	g	G	©	Ì	5	5	%	∞	fi
H	h	H	·	Ó	6	6	^	§	fl
I	i	I	^	È	7	7	&	¶	‡
J	j	J	Δ	Ô	8	8	*	•	°
K	k	K	°	🍎	9	9	(	ª	·
L	l	L	¬	Ò	0	0	)	º	‚
M	m	M	µ	~	`	`	~	`	Ÿ
N	n	N	~	^	-	-	_	–	—
O	o	O	ø	Ø	=	=	+	≠	±
P	p	P	π	∏	[	[	{	"	"
Q	q	Q	œ	Œ	]	]	}	'	'
R	r	R	®	Â	\	\	|	«	»
S	s	S	ß	Í	;	;	:	…	Ú
T	t	T	†	Ê	'	'	"	æ	Æ
U	u	U	¨	Ë	,	,	<	≤	¯
V	v	V	√	◊	.	.	>	≥	˘
W	w	W	Σ	„	/	/	?	÷	¿
X	x	X	≈	Ù	Space Bar				

Desktop Typography with QuarkXPress

Here it is as a keyboard chart.

Chapter 9

Equations and Math

Mathematical symbols are single letters used to designate unknown quantities, variables, and constants. Mathematical symbols are set in italic type, except vectors and tensors, which are generally set in bold face roman type. Numerals, operators, and punctuation are not italic, nor are trigonometric functions or abbreviations. Items set in roman type are preceded and followed by a space.

Rules for math

$\log 2$ *not* $\log 2$

More complicated mathematical material should also be placed within brackets.

$\sin [2p\, (x - y)/n]$

Leave a space before and after mathematical operators that have numbers on both sides.

4×5 cm

When plus and minus signs are used with one number that is not part of an equation, do not leave a space between the sign and the number.

-12 C

Mathematical expressions can be used as part of a sentence when the subject, verb, and object are all part of the mathematical expression.

When $V = 12$, then eq 15 is valid.

However, do not use the equals sign (=) instead of the word "equals" in narrative text. The same applies to the greater than (<) and less than (>) symbols and plus (+) and minus (-) signs.

Form the plurals of mathematical symbols by adding an apostrophe and "s" if you cannot use a word like "values" and "levels."

In equations, leave a space before and after mathematical operators $(+, -, x, =)$ except when they are superscripts or subscripts.

Equations displayed on separate lines should be numbered with Arabic numbers in parentheses placed at the right margin. If an equation is very short and will not be referred to again, it should

Desktop Typography with QuarkXPress

Italic usage with equations

be run into the text and not numbered. Use parentheses in accordance with the rules of mathematics. If the solidus (/) is used in division and if there is any doubt about where the numerator starts or the denominator ends, use parentheses.

Do not use any punctuation after equations displayed on separate lines.

Enclose parentheses within square brackets; enclose square brackets within braces. Do not use square brackets, parentheses, or braces around the symbol to make it represent any other quantity. Use square brackets to denote coordination entities.

Italic type is used for single letters that denote mathematical constants, variables, and unknown quantities in text and in equations. When such single letters become adjective combinations, they are still italic.

Chemical element symbols used to denote attachment to an atom are set in italic type.

Italic letters within square brackets are used to form names for polycyclic aromatic compounds.

In polymer nomenclature, *co, alt, b, g, r,* and *m* are set in italic type when they appear with the chemical name or formula. They are never capitalized.

In the newer polymer nomenclature, the words *block, graft, cross, inter,* and *blend* are italicized when they appear with a chemical name. They are never capitalized.

Italic type is used for symmetry groups and space groups.

Chemical formulas are not italic.

Italic type is not used for common Latin terms and abbreviations.

Structural prefixes "cyclo" and "iso" are set in roman type and are spelled solid (without hyphens or space).

Greek letters, not the spelled-out forms, are used in chemical and drug names. When such names are the first word of a sentence or when they appear in titles or headings, the Greek letter is retained and the first non-Greek roman letter is capitalized.

Small capital letters D and L are used for absolute configuration with amino acids and carbohydrates.

Boldface roman type is used for vectors and tensors. Boldface roman type is used for Arabic compound numbers.

Abbreviate the unit of measure when it appears with a numeral; leave a space between a number and a unit of measure, except when they form a unit modifier, in which case use a hyphen between them.

Spell out the unit of measure when no quantity is given.

Do not use plurals for abbreviated units of measure.

In ranges and series, retain only the final unit of measure.

When a sentence starts with a specific quantity, spell it out as well as the unit of measure.

The next two pages list some of the mathematical symbols and their names:

More rules for math

Desktop Typography with QuarkXPress

⟨ Angle bracket, colloquially 'Bra'

⟩ Angle bracket, colloquially 'Ker'

⟪ Double angle bracket

⟫ Double angle bracket

⟦ Open bracket

⟧ Open bracket

⫽ Italic open bracket

⫽ Italic open bracket

. 1) Full point
2) Scalar product

! Factorial sign

· Decimal point (5 unit)

· Decimal point (9 unit)

∗ Central asterisk

∗∗ Exponent (Fortran)

′ Prime

″ Double prime

‴ Triple prime

⁗ Quadruple prime

‵ Reversed prime

° Degree

∵ Because or since

∴ Therefore, hence

: Sign of proportion

∷ Sign of proportion

∺ Geometric proportion

/ Divided by, solidus

// Tangental to

| 1) Modulus, used thus $|x|$
2) Joint denial, thus $p \mid q$
3) Divides, thus $3 \mid 6$

‖ 1) Parallel to
2) Norm of a function, used thus $\|x\|$
3) Norm of a matrix

∦ Not parallel to

⊥ Necessarily satisfies

≡ 1) Congruent to
2) Definitional identity (math. logic)
3) Identical with
4) Equivalent to (math. logic)

∤ Does not divide

1) Is homothetically congruent to
2) Recursive function

Equal or parallel

⊢ 1) What follows is true, assertion (math. logic)
2) Is deducible from

¬ Logical negation

∨ 1) Disjunction of statements (math. logic)
2) Sum of two sets (math. logic)
3) Logical 'or'

∧ 1) Vector product
2) Product of two sets (math. logic)
3) Symmetric difference of two sets (math. logic)
4) Logical 'and'

∃ There exists

∄ There does not exist

∈ Is an element of

∉ Is not an element of

∉ Is not an element of

∀ For all

□ 1) D'Alembertain operator
2) Mean operator (finite differences)

Γ Gamma function

∂ Partial differentiation

Δ Increment or forward finite difference operator

∇ Nabla or del or backward finite difference operator

∇ Hamilton operator

ϑ Curly theta

∏ Product sign

∑ Summation sign

Ϝ Digamma function

ℵ Aleph. The number of finite integers is $\aleph_0$ and transfinite cardinal numbers $\aleph_1, 2, 3 \ldots$

℘ Weierstrass elliptic function

& Conjunction of statements (math. logic)

ℰ Eulers sign

O Of order, used thus: $O(x)$

o Of lower order than, used thus: $o(x)$

ƒ Function of, used thus: $f(x)$

ℏ Planck Constant over 2π

ℏ Planck Constant over 2π

lim Upper limit

lim Lower limit

lim Limits

⊗ 1) Plethysm operator (group theory)
2) Convolution product
3) Direct product
4) Tensor product

⊗

⊙

∝ Most positive

= 1) Equal to
2) Logical identity

≠ Is not equal to

≠ 1) Is not equal to
2) Logical diversity

≈ 1) Approximately equal to
2) Asymptotic to
3) Equal to in the mean
4) Isomorphism

≉ Not asymptotic to

≊ Approximately equal to or equal to

≑ Approximately equal to

≒ Is the image of

≃ Approximately equal

≅ Approximately equal to or equal to

≥ Greater than or equal to

≥ Greater than or equal to

≧ Greater than or equal to

≱ Not greater than nor equal to

⋛ Less than, equal to, or greater than

⋛ Greater than, equal to, or less than

⋛ Greater than, equal to, or less than

⋚ Less than, greater than, or equal to

⋛ Greater than, less than, or equal to

≥ Equal to or greater than

≐ 1) Approaches the limit
2) Approaches in value to

≑

≒ Estimates or is estimated by

⋀ Is projective with or projective correspondence

⋀ Perspective correspondence

⋁ Equiangular (geometry)

→ 1) Approaches or tends to the limit
2) Implies (math. logic)
3) Referents of a relation (used thus: $\vec{R}$ math. logic)
4) Transformation (set theory)

↔ Does not tend to

← Relata of a relation, used thus $\vec{R}$

↑ 1) Increases monotonically to a limit
2) Exponent (Algol)

↓ Decreases monotonically to a limit

↕

⇒ Implies

⇔ 1) Implies and is implied by
2) If and only if

⇒ Convergence

⇐ Is implied by

↔ 1) Mutually implies
2) One-to-one correspondence with
3) Corresponds reciprocally
4) Asymptotically equivalent to
5) If and only if

↔ Does not mutually imply

↠ On to map (Topology)

↣ 1 – 1 map

⇆

⇄

↻ Clockwise

↺ Anti-clockwise

≻ 1) Has a higher rank or order
2) Contains

⪰ Contains or is equal to

⪰ Is equal to or contains

⪰ Contains or is equal to

≺ Has a lower rank or order

⊀ 1) Has not a lower rank or order than
2) Is not contained in nor equal to

⪯ Is contained in or equal to

⪯ Is contained in or equal to

⋠ Is not contained in nor equal to

⪷ Is contained in or is equivalent to

⋘ Has much lower rank or order

▷ Implies

◁ 1) Implied by

Desktop Typography with QuarkXPress

2) Is a normal sub group of

If and only if

Does not imply

1) Implies
2) Contains as proper sub-set

Contains as proper sub-set

Does not contain

Does not contain

1) Is implied by
2) Contained as proper sub-set within

1) Is not implied by
2) Is not a proper sub-set of

1) Contained as sub-set within
2) Is identical to

Contained as sub-set within

1) Is not contained as sub-set within
2) Is not identical to

Is not contained as sub-set within

1) Contains as sub-set
2) Is identical to

Contains as sub-set

1) Does not contain as sub-set
2) Is not identical to

Contains or is contained in

Is included in, as sub-relation (math. logic)

Includes as sub-relation (math. logic)

1) Empty set
2) Diameter
3) Average value

Non-alternation

Non-alternation

Product or intersection, or meet of two classes (math. logic) or sets (algebra) colloquially 'Cap'

Sum or union or join of two classes (math. logic) or sets (algebra) colloquially 'Cup'

Product of classes or sets between limits, used thus: $\bigcap_{n=m}^{\infty}$

Sum of classes or sets between limits, used thus: $\bigcup_{n=m}^{\infty}$

Non-conjunction

Geometrically equivalent to

Equivalent to

1) Approximately equal to
2) Asymptotically equal
3) Chain homotopic to

Not asymptotically equal

1) Similar to
2) Geometrically equivalent or congruent to
3) Equal or nearly equal to

1) Difference between
2) Is equivalent to
3) Asymptotic to
4) Similar to
5) Of the order of
6) The complement of
7) Is not, negation sign (math. logic)
8) Associate to

1) Is not equivalent to
2) Is not asymptotic to
3) Is not similar to
4) Is not the complement of

Is approximately asymptotic to

Homothetic (similar and perspective to)

Smaller than

Less than

Greater than

Not less than

Not greater than

Equivalent to or greater than

Greater than or equivalent to

Not greater than nor equivalent to

Equivalent to or less than

Less than or equivalent to

Greater than, equivalent to or less than

Less than or approximately equal to

Greater than or approximately equal to

Much less than

Much less than

Much greater than

Much greater than

Not much less than

Not much greater than

Very much less than

Very much greater than

Less than or greater than (is not equal to)

Greater than or less than (is not equal to)

Less than or equal to

Less than or equal to

Less than or equal to

Not less than nor equal to

Congruent and parallel

Smash product

1) Between
2) Quantic, no numerical coefficients

Infinity

Not infinite

Varies as, proportional to

Radical sign

End of operation of radical sign (reverse slash)

Plus

Minus

Multiply

Divide

Plus or minus

Minus or plus

Direct sum (group theory)

Direct sum (group theory)

Rotation in negative direction

Rotation in positive direction

Plus or equal

Equal or plus

Nim-addition

Positive difference or sum

Sum or positive difference

Symmetric difference

Integral

1) Contour integral
2) Closed line integral

Double contour integral

Contour integral (anti-clockwise)

Contour integral (clockwise)

Circulation function

Finite part integral

Line integration by rectangular path around a pole

Line integration by semi-circular path around a pole

Line integration not including the pole

Line integration including the pole

Quarternion integral

Element of construction

Element of construction

Angle

Spherical angle

1) Orthogonal to
2) Perpendicular to

Parenthesis

Parenthesis

Bracket

Bracket

Brace

Brace

Chapter 10

Pi Characters

Pi characters and pi fonts refer to individual symbols and collections of special characters such as math or monetary symbols or decorative symbols.

∨⇔⇐⇑⇑⇒⇓◊Υ⟨®∇±≅#∃⊥∗()_+∈©™∑⌠⌈⌋↓÷©∪⌊⌊⌊∪⟩∫→⌈⌉

In handset metal type, *pi* refers to type of one style mistakenly put in the storage drawer of another style, and by extension any mixup of type.

When setting hand-set type the composer might run across an "m" that didn't match the face he was using. He would throw this orphan into a box of "pi" type to be either sorted out later or sent back to the type foundry for credit toward buying a new font.

Special characters. Typesetting systems offer a host of specialized characters not normally found on a typewriter keyboard. Most typographic systems offer a selection of pi characters, usually on a different "level" of the keyboard. They are accessed by using a special shift (Option, for example) or code key. (⌘ in Macintosh programs). The regular shift key allows you to type upper and lowercase letters using the same typewriter key. The additional shift keys and combinations of shift and code keys provide access to additional characters.

The inch symbol as quote marks. Typists use vertical double (") quote marks; publishers use open (") and close (") quote marks. To set a double open quote on a Macintosh keyboard, type the **Option-[** combination; for a double close quote, type the **Option-Shift-[** combination.

The foot symbol as single quote marks. Typists use a vertical (') quote mark; publishers use open (') and close (') quote marks. On a Macintosh keyboard, type **Option-]** for an open single quote; type **Option-Shift-]** for a single close quote.

The foot symbol as apostrophe. Typists use the foot symbol ('); publishers use an apostrophe, typed as a close single quote mark.

Double hyphens as a dash. Publishers use the hyphen, en dash, and em dash where appropriate. Use hyphens in words broken at line ends and between compound words. Use em dashes to indicate an abrupt change in thought — like this. Use en dashes where appropriate. On a Macintosh keyboard, type **Option-hyphen** for an en dash; type **Option-Shift-hyphen** for an em dash. Typing

Special symbols

Desktop Typography with QuarkXPress

Option-space (hit the space bar once) creates a breaking en space; ⌘**Option-space** creates a non-breaking en space.

Points of Ellipsis

Three dots as points of ellipsis. Points of ellipsis are characters made up of three dots that indicate that words were intentionally left out. Publishers should use the special ellipsis character, since spacing between individually typed periods can change from line to line depending upon word and letter spacing.If the ellipsis is used for words dropped from the end of a sentence, use the ellipsis character followed by a normal period. To create an ellipsis on a Macintosh keyboard, type the **Option-;** combination.

Bullets

The asterisk or a lowercase "o" colored in as a bullet. Real publishers use real bullets. On a Macintosh keyboard, type **Option-8** to create a bullet.

To summarize:

Option-[produces "
Option-] produces '

Option-Shift-[produces "
Option-Shift-] produces '

Option-hyphen produces –
Option-Shift-hyphen produces —

Option-; produces …

Option-8 produces •

Dingbats

Symbols and decorative elements. These characters are also called "dingbats." The samples below are from the Zapf Dingbats font.

✳ ❋ ✽ ➁ ✺ ☽ ✖ ✎ ❑ ✐ ✛ ✲ ❖ ❘ ■ ✳ ✗

Boxes and bullets

The two most common non-character characters used in typography are boxes and bullets:

Boxes (or Squares)	❑ (Open)	■ (Closed)
Bullets	○ (Open)	● (Closed)

Boxes and bullets should be as close to the x-height as possible if used full size, centered on the x-height if they're set smaller.

More often than not, you will have to change the point size of boxes and bullets so they optically match the x-height.

The "Option-8" bullet in the Adobe fonts used for most Macintosh printing (•) is relatively small. The "Unshift L" (●) bullet in the Zapf Dingbats font is rather large.

•xH
The Option 8 bullet at text size (12 point)

●xH
The Unshift L bullet at text size (12 point)

•xH
The Option 8 bullet slightly larger (14 point)

●xH
The Unshift L bullet slightly smaller(9 point)

For keyboarding efficiency you are better off using the Option-8 bullet at the text size. If you're a stickler for details, the Option-8 bullet slightly larger than normal is better.

Agate: Originally, the sizes of type were expressed in names, not numbers. The name for 5.5-point type was Agate, and it is still used to describe the point size often used for newspaper classified advertising.

Agate

Two agate lines of type. Set at 5.5 point. The fonts for agate classified work were specially designed for legibility at small sizes. Fonts such as Ionic, Opticon and Spartan were used for classified advertising.

Newspapers also use "agate" as a unit of measurement for display advertising. There are 14 "agate" lines in 1 inch. Ad rates are usually "per line, per column." Thus a 2-column, 2-inch ad would be 56 "lines" (2 x 4 x 12 = 56).

A note about classifieds. Classified ads, or "liners," are separated by rule lines. The column width depends upon the publication. Never assume a column width; always confirm its value.

Calligraphy means "beautiful writing" and is also a form of *hand lettering*, which is the drawing of letters by hand. Typography is lettering adapted and made more orderly for special purposes, such as a mechanical reproduction.

Calligraphic characters

The "Chancery" script of the 15th Century became the model for our *italics*, and the writing masters of the period — Palatino, for one — developed techniques for formal handwriting.

Zapf Chancery

A calligraphic typeface based on the Renaissance "Chancery"

Superiors and inferiors

Superior and inferior characters are usually set in a smaller point size than the accompanying typeface and are positioned above (superiors) and below (inferiors) the baseline. They are also called subscripts (inferior) and superscripts (superior). There can also be super superscripts and sub subscripts and a few in between. They are used for:

1. Chemical equations
2. Math equations
3. Footnote references

They are most often numerals, but alphabetic characters are sometimes used as well.

Superiors and inferiors can be "manufactured" by changing to a smaller size and advancing or reversing line spacing (if this capability is available) for positioning. Sometimes it's called "jumping the baseline."

Both superior and inferior figures should be set at least two sizes smaller using the same face as the body copy.

$H^{1234567890ABCabc}$ $H_{1234567890ABCabc}$

Superior or Superscript   **Inferior or Subscript**

Superior figures should be raised from the baseline at least 3 points. Inferior figures should be set below the baseline at least 2 points.

There should be no space *before* superior and inferior numbers and no space *after* an inferior number if it is a middle part of a physical, chemical, or mathematical expression.

The use of inferior and superior characters and symbols is also called exponential notation.

Some typesetting equipment will not have smaller figures on its fonts for setting footnote numbers or mathematical and scientific formulas. These rules apply if this is the case.

Asterisks, daggers, and double daggers are set in the same font as body copy and do not require any vertical adjustments. They may also be used as superiors. The order in which these symbols should be used is as follows: the first footnote appears with an asterisk, the second footnote a dagger, and the third footnote a double dagger. Using two or more asterisks together is rarely done because it appears too bulky. If there are more than three footnotes, use numbers—beginning with the number 1.

The symbols © and ® are legal necessities in some copy. They can be created using the Macintosh keyboard as follows:

Copyright symbols

®   TM   ©

Option-r   **Option-2**   **Option-g**

These symbols should be proportional in size to the text that they accompany.

H®   H™   H©

Normal size

H®   H™   H©

As superiors

Ligatures are two or more characters designed as a distinct unit. They should be used sparingly in headlines. There are five f-ligatures plus the diphthongs. Gutenberg's font had many "ligatures" in order to simulate handwriting.

Ligatures

fi fl

Individual letters

fi fl

Ligatures

Although ligatures are often mandatory in book production, they're rarely useful in advertising typography. In fact, they cannot be used in copy set tighter than normal spacing. The Macintosh keyboard lets you define the fi and fl ligatures.

Option-Shift-5 produces fi
Option-Shift-6 produces fl

Dipthongs

Eventually automation will allow *any* ligature to be selected without operator intervention — an incentive for the expansion of ligature design and use — until we someday return to a modern version of the Gutenberg font.

The diphthongs æ and œ, Æ and Œ, are also considered ligatures.

æ oe AE OE

æ œ Æ Œ

Symbol font

The most commonly used pi collection used in the Macintosh world is the Symbol font. In most situations, you only need one symbol; you must still go through the menu route to change fonts back and forth.

 With QuarkXPress you can instantly access the Symbol font by typing **Control-Shift-q** — the next character typed will be a pi character.

The following examples are the Symbol font complements. The top row of each section is the unshift, followed by the Shift, Option, and Option-Shift levels. The samples start from the top row of the keyboard (the line of keys with numerals) and proceed to the lowest row.

1234567890–=

!≅#∃%⊥&*()_+

ℑ♠≤′%ƒ∞≈…∠↑

∨⇔⇐⇑⇒⇓◊ϒ〈®∇±

θωερτψυιοπ[].∴

ΘΩΕΡΤΨΥΙΟΠ{}|

∉•↔♦×←⊥⌙≠®™∩

∈©™Σ⌠|⌈↓÷©∏∪

ασδφγηφκλ;϶

ΑΣΔΦΓΗϑΚΛ:∀

♣∂⊗♥|∅⌋ℜ⊃—

|⌊⌡⌈⌊⟩⌡→

ζξχϖβνμ,./

ΖΞΧςΒΝΜ<>?

|⊕℘≡~∝″≥√

⌈|·⌡⟩⌡⌠ℵ

Chapter 11

Punctuation

Desktop Typography with QuarkXPress

One of the first printers to break up text with punctuation was Manutius shortly before 1500. The period indicated a full stop at the end of a sentence, and the / was used as a comma is used today to indicate a pause in reading. The semicolon was introduced in England in the late 1500s.

The question mark, or "query," from the Latin *quaestio* (for "what"), was represented as a Q with a small o under it and came to England in 1521. The exclamation point, also called a "screamer" and a "bang," from the Latin *Io* (for "joy"), was represented as an I with a small o under it and arrived in England at the same time as the question mark.

Question marks

The apostrophe is used in contractions, abbreviations, and to form possessives. It is optional in plural abbreviations or numerals:

Apostrophes

> MDs or MD's
> 1980s . . . but should be added to avoid ambiguity:
> "Give me all the a's."

An apostrophe is *one* close quote; close quotes are *two apostrophes.*

Prime   Option-] (Apostrophe)   Two apostrophes   Option Shift-] (Close Quotes)

Additional space at the ends of sentences is called "French Spacing." It is a very old practice, having been commonplace in books up through the 19th century. It is analogous to typewritten copy in which two full word spaces are placed at the end of the sentence.

French spacing

In typesetting, a space about one-quarter of the em in width in addition to a word space was used for setting "French Spacing." The practice is difficult to implement today, although computer systems will be able to automate it. The extra space must be truncated at the end of a line, which could make word spacing erratic. Many computer typesetting systems automatically take out double word spaces because the resultant spaces vary widely in width.

Hanging punctuation in the margin to create optical justification is a seemingly modern practice. However, in the Gutenberg Bible, hyphens were "hung" in the margin. So much for progress. In most cases, the punctuation hangs in the right margin.

Punctuation, past and present

In quite early fonts the slash was used for the comma, or more accurately, it was used to indicate any short pause in reading. The modern comma was introduced into England about 1521 (in Roman type) and 1535 (in Blackletter). It appeared in Venetian printing before 1500.

The semicolon seems to have been first used in England about 1569, but it was not common until about 1580.

The period, or full stop, was commonly used *before* as well as *after* roman, and sometimes Arabic, numerals until about 1580. Thus you might see notations such as ".xii."

The single quotes (' and ') were used commonly in such abbreviations as th' for "the." It may be noted that t'is (instead of 'tis) was so common in the Elizabethan period that it should perhaps be regarded as normal.

All punctuation marks should be printed in the same style or font of type as the word, letter, character, or symbol immediately preceding them. Italic or boldface parentheses and brackets should not be used if the beginning parenthesis or bracket was in the regular font. Is there such a thing as an italic period? Not really.

Is there an italic period?

● ● **The period on the left is normal; the other is italic**

- Double punctuation is not used except with quotes, parentheses, and brackets.
- All except ending punctuation should be dropped before a closing parenthesis.
- End punctuation in a syllabus and similar material should be consistent: if there are one or more complete sentences, periods should be used after all entries; if there are no complete sentences, omit periods.
- Neither a comma nor a dash is ever retained before a parenthetical element (unless the parentheses are used to mark divisions of enu-

merations run into the text).

- If needed in the sentence, the comma or the dash is transferred to follow the closing parenthesis.

Parentheses

Parentheses are used in pairs except when enumerated divisions are paragraphed. A single parenthesis is ordinarily used to follow a lowercase (italic) letter or a lowercase roman numeral, for example *a)*; a period is used with Arabic figures and capital (roman) letters. Parentheses have traditionally been called "thumbnails."

In syllabi and similar material, parentheses and other characters adhere to the following scheme of indention:

I. Under the head of . . .
  A. Under . . .
    1. Under . . .
      a) Under . . .
        (1) Under . . .
          (a) Under . . .
            i) Under . . .
            ii) Under . . .
          (b) Under . . .
        (2) Under . . .
      b) Under . . .
    2. Under . . .
  B. Under . . .
II. Under the head of . . .

Multiples of en spaces were used to accomplish the example above.

Parentheses should not ordinarily be used for parenthetical clauses unless confusion might arise from the use of less distinctive marks or unless the content of the clause is irrelevant to the sentence.

Rules for parentheses:

- In correct usage, parenthetical expressions contain information that is subsidiary to the point that the sentence is making. The sentence does not depend on the information within the parentheses.
- A parenthetical expression is a stop sign to the reader, indicating a change in tone, an aside, a running footnote if you will.
- Use parentheses for parenthetical expressions that clarify, identify, or illustrate and that direct the reader.

Desktop Typography with QuarkXPress

- Use parentheses to enumerate.
- Use parentheses in pairs, not singly, except as in 1), 2), etc., for lists.
- If items are numbered for future citing in text, do not put the numbers in parentheses. Such numbers are not parenthetical.
- Do not use parentheses when citing a reference or equation in a narrative. In this case, the reference or equation number is the point of the sentence. It's not subsidiary information and thus not parenthetical.
- Use parentheses to identify the trademark and manufacturer of reagents and equipment.
- If a parenthetical sentence is within another sentence, do not use a final period for the sentence in parentheses.
- If a parenthetical sentence is not within another sentence, use a final period inside the closing parenthesis.
- Enclose oxidation numbers within parentheses, closed up to the element name or symbol, in text but not in formulas. (In formulas use superscripts.)

The parentheses and punctuation rule states that punctuation marks can be set either inside or outside of parentheses, depending on whether the sentence or clause using the punctuation *began* inside or outside the parentheses.

Punctuation marks should be in the same style and weight as the face of the phrase or clause to which the punctuation refers. General practice is different, however. It has now become acceptable to many editors to punctuate in the same face as the preceding word.

Some rules for placing punctuation:

Periods:
- When a period is used with closing quotation marks, place it inside the quote marks. This is proper, but do not change the location of quote marks if punctuation is consistently placed outside in a manuscript. If the manuscript is inconsistent, make all quoted material the same with the period inside.

Ellipses:
- Points of ellipsis should have fixed spaces between the points. A fixed space should follow the last ellipsis point if the ellipsis indicates an omission in a sentence.

If the ellipsis indicates that more follows the sentence but it is followed by a new sentence (which starts with a capital letter), a regular word space follows the last point of the ellipsis. If the omission occurs at the end of a sentence, a fourth point is used — the period for that sentence. In this case, the first point is set as a period (no space between the word and period), and the three points of the ellipsis are set with space between.

Em and en dashes:
- Use an em dash to separate parenthetical thoughts in a sentence.
- Use an en dash to mean "through" or "to" as in "grades K–2" and "1978–1980;" do not use a hyphen. An en dash should not begin a line of type. It is permissible, however, for a line to end with an en dash (as if it were a hyphen).
- Em dashes may be open or closed, that is, with or without space on either side. Different publications use different styles. Whatever you do, make sure you don't end up with a line that starts with an em dash.

Brackets:
- Use brackets to enclose parenthetical matter within material already included in parentheses. Brackets should be used within parentheses, not outside (except in algebraic equations).

Headlines follow most punctuation rules with a few exceptions:

- Periods are only used in abbreviations.
- Quotation marks are always single, not double.
  For example: **Mayor says 'no'**
- Commas often replace the word *and*.
- Semicolons may separate two related thoughts just as they might in text copy. Use them only in a headline that runs two or more lines.

Quotes

Quotes are opening and closing punctuation marks that indicate verbal statements or define or emphasize certain words. Double quotes are generally used. Single quotes are used within a double quote, as in "doubles on the outside, 'singles' on the inside." The single close quote is also an apostrophe.

Quotation marks (quotes) were originally commas. In the 1600s they looked like the present so-called French Quotes (<< >>) and were placed in the center of the type body so that the same character could be used for either the open or closed position.

English printers refused to use the French form. They inverted the comma at the beginning of quoted matter and used the apostrophes at the close. Of course, they were not symmetrical. It has long been recommended that a hair space (less than one third of an en space — accomplished using positive letterspacing units in current typesetting systems) be used to separate the quotes from certain letters:

$$H" \quad H" \quad H"$$

Left is normal spacing; center is –6 units; right +6 units

Set all quotations of passages in the author's own words that are run into the text within quotation marks (quotes). When quoting consecutive paragraphs of the same work, repeat quotation marks at the beginning of each paragraph; use close quotes only at the end of the last paragraph quoted.

In French and Spanish, small angle marks on the lower part of the type body are used for quotation marks; in German, two primes on one type body are used, the opening quote being inverted. (Foreign quotations in roman type, however, when run into English text, are introduced and finished with the usual English quotation marks.) In Spanish and French texts long dashes and paragraph breaks may be used in lieu of quotation marks to introduce successive speeches.

Quotes, again

When passages are quoted from other authors or from different works of the same author and are not separated by intervening original matter, each passage should be set within quotation marks unless the passages are set in smaller type. If they are set smaller, quotation marks should be omitted, and the passages should be separated from one another by extra leading.

The procedure for altering quoted material: When an author alters a quoted word to change a letter from a cap to a lowercase (or the reverse), the word is typeset with brackets—not parentheses—around the altered letter, such as [w]ord (meaning it originally had a capital W). This procedure may also be used when an author adds letters, words, or phrases to quoted material, such as

"Things were not the same [in the beginning]." (meaning the last phrase was added to the quote).

Indenting quoted material: Quotes that run longer than five lines if set in the regular body typeface should be set apart from the rest of the body copy. The following rules apply to setting quoted matter apart from body text:

- Set the quoted material one size smaller than the body face. Make sure leading is no more than 2 extra points greater than your quote type size. This kind of separated text is also called an "extract."
- Indent 2 picas maximum from both left and right margins. In some publications, long quoted material is indented 2 picas from the left only—with the right margin remaining the same as the body copy.
- Inserting extra points of leading before and after the quoted material is a matter of style. Sometimes extra leading is used for appearance, but you should never add as much as one complete line of white space.
- When quoted material is indented, it no longer begins and ends with quote marks. Setting the quote apart from the body eliminates the need for quote marks. You may have to change the manuscript to reflect the absence of open and close quotes. Any single quotes appearing within the quoted section will become double quotes.
- Paragraph indents in quoted matter should be indented one additional em space.
- Significant omissions of copy in a long quote section (significant meaning whole paragraphs or sections) is sometimes shown by asterisks rather than by points of ellipsis. To set asterisks for this purpose, add 4 to 6 points lead before the next line of copy, which will be three asterisks centered with two fixed spaces between each asterisk. Continue on the next line with the following line of copy. Asterisks showing omitted copy do not appear on the same typeset line as copy; points of ellipsis should be used in these instances.
- Setting quotes apart with indents doesn't work with narrow columns (such as newspaper columns). There is not enough room to indent and reduce size. Simply set quoted matter as text copy, with quote marks.
- Usually, the punctuation at the end of a quote negates the need for additional space at the close.

Desktop Typography with QuarkXPress

Regarding punctuation at the end of a quotation, the rule is: All punctuation marks [. , ; : ? !] come before end quote marks. If there are end single and double quote marks together, set the single quote, punctuation, then double quote marks in that order.

The exception is: In legal and insurance material, the placement of punctuation marks can make a difference in meaning, which could result in a lawsuit. Use punctuation marks as the originator wants them and let the chips fall where they may.
Here are some rules for quote marks:

- Place closing quotation marks before all punctuation that is not part of the original quotation. Place them after all punctuation that is part of the quotation.
- Use double quotation marks for new words, words used in a new sense, and words not used literally, but only the first time they appear in the text.
- Use quotation marks to enclose short, direct quotations (two or three sentences).
- Use a narrower page width and no quotation marks for longer quotations (extracts) of 50 words or more.
- Use single quotation marks only when they are within double quotation marks.

Commas

The comma causes a great deal of trouble for something so small. Here are some rules regarding the use of commas:

- Use a comma before and after Jr. and Sr. No comma is necessary with II and III, as in John Smith III.
- Use a comma after the day in a date. Don't use one after the month when the day is not given.
- Within a sentence, use a comma after the year as well, as in "On July 23, 1988, this book … .
- In a series of words or phrases containing three or more items, use commas before "and" and "or."
- Use a comma before the coordinating conjunctions "and," "or," "nor," "but," "yet," "for," and "so" connecting two main clauses (complete thoughts).
- Use commas to set off "that is," "namely," and "for example."
- Within a sentence use commas between city and state and after state, as in "He has lived in Denver, Colorado, for eight years."

- In parenthetical expressions, use a comma before and after "i.e." and "e.g."
- Do not use a comma before "et al."

Rules for colons:

Colons

- Use a colon to introduce a word, phrase, list, complete sentence, or several complete sentences that illustrate, clarify, or expand the information that precedes it.
- Use a colon to express numerical ratios. A slant (solidus) is also acceptable.
- Do not use a colon (or any punctuation) between a verb and its object or a preposition and its object.

The slash or solidus also has some rules:

Slash

- Use a solidus for simple fractions and all subscript and superscript fractions.
- Use a solidus as a symbol for "per" in abbreviated units of measure.
- Do not use a slash (solidus) between words in text. Using the solidus to mean "and" or "or" is not recommended by authoritative style guides. For example, in "and/or" the solidus means "or," but this combination is much overused. Closer reading of the text often reveals that either "and" or "or" is sufficient. Furthermore, an en dash is the preferred punctuation to mean "and."

Rules for the lowly period:

Period

- Do not use periods after abbreviated units of measure and most other abbreviations and symbols except when the abbreviation could be confused with another word (example: in. for inches, at. for atomic, no. for number).
- Use periods between numbers within square brackets for form names for bridged and spiro alicyclic compounds.

There are rules for brackets, too:

Brackets

- Use square brackets within quotation marks to form names for polycyclic aromatic compounds.
- Use numbers separated by periods within square brackets to form names of bridged and spiro alicyclic compounds.
- Use square brackets closed up to the compound name to indicate isotopic labeling.

Desktop Typography with QuarkXPress

More rules for brackets

The bracket is also used in pairs within a sentence to mark interjected words of explanation or comment (usually made by author, reporter, or editor) that seem necessary for a better understanding of the subject. Brackets that enclose many sentences indicate passages of inferior importance that may be omitted or that need not be made a part of the text. This occurs most frequently in newspaper reports of speeches, as in the following example:

> We would have our Union to be a union of hearts, and we would have our Constitution obeyed, not merely because force compels that obedience, but obeyed because the people love the principles of the Constitution [long-continued applause]; and today, if I am called to the work to which Abraham Lincoln was called sixteen years ago, it is under brighter skies and more favorable auspices. [Applause.]

In the example above, the enclosures in brackets are obviously by the reporter. In a reprint of a misspelled or badly worded letter, the obvious errors are pointed out by enclosing in brackets the corrections of the mistakes.

> I want you to no [know] that I don't think you can't learn [teach] my boys ennythink [anything] about gramer or speling.

Sometimes no attempt is made to correct misspellings. The error can be noted by putting [sic] or [so] after the misspelled word.

The bracket is employed in legal or ecclesiastical papers where numerical words have to be changed to suit varying conditions, and where details have to be supplied, as in

> This is the first [second or third] time of asking. The directors of this society shall be six in number, and shall remain in office [here state the time], and no longer.

One bracket is also used to enclose an ending word of a line of poetry that will not come within the measure and must be turned over or taken back in the preceding short line.

> Weary knife-grinder! little think the proud ones,
> Who in their coaches roll along the turnpike [and
> Road, what hard work 'tis crying all day, "Knives
> Scissors to grind O!"

The bracketing in a previous line of a word too long for the line was common in old printing, but it is justifiable now only when it saves space.

Sometimes the bracket is used to prevent the confusion that results when parentheses are placed within parentheses. Sterne used them freely for this purpose.

> I know the banker I deal with, or the physician I
> usually call in—[There is no need, cried Dr. Slop
> (waking) to call in any physician in this case] —
> to be neither of them men of much religion.

Publishers are sometimes at a loss when it comes to deciding when to use parentheses and when to use brackets. The following general rule will apply in most instances:

> Parentheses always enclose remarks apparently made by the writer of the text. Brackets enclose remarks certainly made by the editor or reporter of that text.

Gutenberg's Bible had hanging punctuation

Chapter 12

Letters

Letters are the basic building blocks of language. Typography deals with the letterform.

The following terms refer specifically to the letterform itself:

Apex: This is the top junction of two stems and is most often evident in the point of the capital A and the center of the capital W. The opposite of an apex—that is the bottom junction of two stems—is the *vortex*. Our cap W has one apex and two vortex points:

Apex

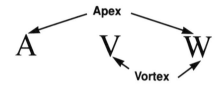

The inside of an apex or vortex is a "crotch."

Ascender: Ascending characters are b, d, f, h, k, l and t. They rise above the x-height and may not always align (although most do) at the top. Because the law of averages says that ascenders from one line will be proximate to descenders from another line, you must select your leading carefully.

Ascender

gjpqy
bdfhklt

gjpqy
bdfhklt

You should be careful to make line spacing or leading sufficiently large so that the ascenders of one line do not touch the descenders of the line above.

In Old Roman and other typefaces the ascenders are sometimes taller than the caps.

HdbH   HdbH   HdbH
Palatino   **Garamond**   **Times**

The descending characters are g, j, p, q and y. They descend below the baseline and usually align at the bottom.

Descenders

Typefaces are designed with descenders to meet the designer's creative feeling—thus some may be shorter (or longer) than others.

Biform: Biform refers to the intermingling of modified small caps and lowercase characters in the formation of a lowercase alphabet. Type set with such characters has a unique appearance. The most famous biform face is "Peignot," illustrated below:

AbcdEfGHijklMNOPQRSTUVWXYZ
ABCDEFGHIJKLMNOPQRSTUVWXYZ

Biforms are most often used in heads, subheads, and advertising display. They are rarely used in text—unless you happen to be an 11th century scribe. Biforms are derived from the uncial versions of handwritten styles.

Blackletter: This term refers to the typefaces derived from the German writing hand of the 13th century. Type of this style is sometimes called "Textura" since it appears to "weave a texture" on the page. It is also called Spire-Gothic and "Old English," as well. (In the past, Americans also used the word gothic as a synonym for sans serif.) Blackletter typefaces were used in Germany until the 1930s.

abcdefghijklmnopqrsſtuv

Bracketed: This term describes the linking of the main stem of a character (vertical) to the serif (horizontal). Bracketing may be "fine" or "full" depending upon the amount of attachment.

I I I

The first two letters are bracketed; the last is not

A square serif typeface is called an "Egyptian," but when it is bracketed it is a "Clarendon" Most "Old Roman" style and "Transitional" Romans are bracketed, but "Modern" Romans, such as Bodoni, are not.

"Egyptian" typefaces derive their names (Cairo, Memphis,

Biform

Blackletter

Bracketed

Karnak, etc.) from the Egyptian campaign of Napoleon, who supposedly used these very readable characters on large sign boards for long-distance message relay using telescopes. They are also called "square" or "slab" serifs. The following example is Lubalin Graph:

Egyptian

ABCDEFGHijklmnopqrstuvwxyz

Brush: This term refers to typefaces that appear to have been drawn with a brush or broad-pointed pen. A casual or informal feeling results from the use of "brush" faces. They are used for greeting cards and special-purpose promotions and occasionally to simulate a handwritten message, although a more formal "script" may be more appropriate.

Brush

abcdefff fifl ghijklmnopqrstuvwxyz
ABCDEFGHIJKL MNOPQRS

Cap Line: A cap line is an imaginary line defining the height of the capital letters of a particular typeface. Capitals can be higher or lower than ascending characters. In Old (Roman) Style typefaces, the capitals are shorter than the ascenders.

Cap Line

bHhHxHyHzHMxHyHxHtHd

Copperplate: This type style dates back to the days of copperplate engraving (an older form of printing). Copperplate type has fine serifs at the ends of all strokes. Instead of using pens or brushes, copperplate engraving was done on a fine polished copper plate with a steel scribe.

Copperplate

ABCDEFGHIJKLMNOPQRSTUVWXYZ
& – 1234567890$
ABCDEFGHIJKLMNOPQRSTUVWXYZ&

In order to get good, sharp corners on the strokes, a final scribe was made perpendicular to the main stroke and was allowed to extend just a bit beyond, creating the copperplate serifs. After printing, and in small point sizes, copperplate serifs often became indistinguishable
Copperplate typefaces do not usually have lowercase characters, using smaller-sized caps instead. These typefaces are used primarily for business cards and business stationery. Copperplate

should *never* be used for text paragraphs.

Counter

Counter: Counter refers to the fully or partially enclosed part of a letter, as in the lowercase *e*, that has a full counter above and a partial below. Counter refers to the *space*, whereas the term "bowl" refers to the lines enclosing the counter.

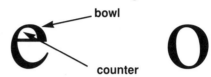

A "complete" bowl is formed by curved strokes only; on a "modified" bowl, a stem forms one of the sides. A "loop" is a bowl that serves as a flourish, for example, the descending part of some lowercase g characters.

Hairline

Hairline: A hairline is the thinnest possible line that can be printed. Typeface characters may include hairline elements, such as stems and serifs, especially in script typefaces.

Be careful when using hairlines; make sure you consider the printing technology that will be used. Reverses and overprints of type with hairline elements present problems.

Inline

Inline: A type style that has a chiseled effect as if chipped out of stone is called inline. The letters are classic in their appearance and should be used in small doses for major display purposes. They are especially well suited to drop out from a dark background.

ABCDEFGHIJKLMNOPQR

Script

Script: Script refers to typefaces designed with connecting characters in imitation of fine handwriting; it should never be used in all caps. There are various levels of script ranging from informal styles (Brush) to Spencerian styles. All are calligraphic in nature.

Desktop Typography with QuarkXPress

Stem: The stem is the main vertical stroke or principal stroke in an oblique character or face. It is the dominant element in most characters. Other elements that are perpendicular to the stem, connected to it, or joined with other main parts of the letterform are:

> **Arm.** A horizontal stroke starting from the stem, as in the capital letter E or F.
>
> **Bar.** An arm connected on both sides, as in the cap H.
>
> **Crossbar.** A horizontal stroke that crosses through the stem, as in the lowercase t. The capital T stroke is actually two arms.
>
> **Bar.** A short stroke extending from the bowl of lowercase g and the stem of the lowercase r.
>
> **Tail.** A downward sloping short stroke, ending free.
>
> The outer portion of the arms and serifs of the letters E, F, G, T, and Z is called a *beak*.

Any curved stroke that is *not* a bowl, is an arc. A "spine" is the main curved (arc) section of the letter S.

Stress: This term refers to the gradation in curved strokes from thick to thin.

Terminal: This is a free ending stroke with one of the special treatments described below:

> *Acute*— angle of acute accent.
> *Concave*— Rounded, out.
> *Convex*— Rounded, in.
> *Flared*— Extended.
> *Grave*— At angle of grave accent.
> *Hook*— Looped.
> *Pointed*— To a point.
> *Sheared*— Sliced off.
> *Straight*— Even.
> *Tapered*— Graduated.

Stem

Stress

Terminal

The "finial" is another form of a terminal that can be an alternative ending. There are several forms:

Beak— Most often a half serif.
Barb— At end of an arc.
Swash— Flourished.

Trap

Trap: This is a compensating indentation cut into the intersection of strokes on a letter. Particularly in phototypesetting and especially on bold faces, the problem of "bleed" arises frequently, because of changes in focus, light exposure intensity, and even bleed of ink in printing. If any of these factors are off, the intersection of strokes on the character can become rounded instead of sharp.

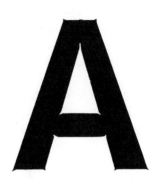

To compensate for this bleeding, "traps" are cut in the problem areas. When printed, photographic and ink bleed spread the intersection out to where it optically belongs. Often, a character may be redesigned several times before the ideal trap for it is determined. One problem with traps is that they often show up when type is set in large point sizes.

Uncial

Uncial: This term is derived from the Latin word for crooked, "uncus." An uncial was a capital letter that rounded the straight lines. Uncials were essentially "biform" characters that evolved during the transition from capitals to lowercase as scribes tried to writer faster and faster.

uncials

Closed and Open

Closed: This refers to a character or symbol that is essentially "filled in" or solid. The opposite of closed is *open*, which describes a character or symbol that exists as an outline or is "hollow."

Open   Closed

In the case of en and em dashes, closed refers to the absence of space on either end of the dash; open means that there is a space.

Some publishers prefer open dashes to allow the printer or computer software typesetting program more places to end lines. Since a word space might be too wide and a fixed space might make the combination unacceptable for line termination, you should kern the word space to half of its optimum value. This suggestion does not apply to sophisticated publishing systems, especially those that recognize the dash as an appropriate end-of-line break point.

Outline: This refers to typeface with no guts. Outline faces are used for display work. They lend themselves to colored or tinted layouts, allowing the type to be "dropped out" of the background.

Outline

Outline

Shaded: Shaded typefaces are designed with a third dimension, a drop shadow or a drop outline. This type lends itself to two-color display applications. Drop shadows should be used sparingly.

Drop Shadow

Shaded

Condensed: This refers to characters in a type style that have been squeezed into narrower shapes. Condensed typefaces are used when large amounts of copy must fit into a relatively small space. They are especially useful for setting tabular material

Condensed

Normal   Condensed
100%   70%

There are even gradations of condensation:

- ultra-condensed
- extra-condensed
- condensed
- semi-condensed

The words "narrow" and "compressed" are sometimes used as synonyms for these levels of condensing.

Condensed 25%
Condensed 30%
Condensed 40%
Condensed 50%
Condensed 60%

Digitized printers and typesetters can modify raster lines to create the typographic effect of condensing. Some PC publishing programs accomplish this by allowing you to define new character widths. Thus, 12-point characters can be specified so that they are 80 percent of their normal width

Expanded

Expanded. This term usually refers to the width of all characters in a particular type style. Expanded faces are often used for heads, sub-heads and small blocks of ad copy. This is a variation in width.

Normal Expanded
100%   120%

There are gradations:

- semi-expanded
- expanded
- extra-expanded
- ultra-expanded

Condensed and expanded are subjective terms. The words "extended" and "wide" are often used as synonyms. Note that "Century Expanded," for example, is expanded in the "x-height" direction, not in its width.

Expanded 200%
Expanded 300%
Expand 400%

**Scaling type
with QuarkXPress**

In QuarkXPress, condensing (and expanding) type is accomplished with the **Horiz Scale** menu command under the **Style** menu. Select the type you want scaled; select the **Horiz Scale** command. The horizontal scale dialog box will appear. In the Horiz scale text field you can enter any value between 25 percent and 400 percent.

There is a difference between condensed characters created by a type designer (who creates an entire condensed type face) and characters condensed optically (by lenses) or digitally by machines. The differences are not usually apparent to the uneducated eye, and as a result most typeface variations—condensed and expanded—are machine-created.

Remember, in a condensed typeface the em space is still a square formed by the value of the point size. Thus, fixed widths will appear wider than normal. However, if you "condense" a typeface by changing the set width, then all values will change, even the fixed spaces.

Digitized typesetters can modify character "set width" electronically to create wider spacing *between* characters. This is is different from expanding and condensing the type. In this case, space is added or subtracted between characters—technically, letterspacing.

Set width

With QuarkXPress you can adjust width without affecting type using the **Track/Kern** menu command under the **Style** menu. Select the text you want to make narrower or wider. Select the **Track** menu command (which is available when a range of text is selected). In the Track dialog box you can enter any value between -100 and 100, depending on the amount of space you want between letters. Negative values tighten spacing; positive values create additional space. Kerning is available when the insertion bar is between characters. By inserting negative values in the Kern dialog box, you can tighten the space between character pairs. The example below shows the set width increasing from normal (0 tracking) to 16 in four unit increments:

Adjusting width with QuarkXPress

abcdefgABCDEFGhijklmnHIJKLMNopqrstuv
abcdefgABCDEFGhijklmnHIJKLMNopqrstuv
abcdefgABCDEFGhijklmnHIJKLMNopqrstuv
abcdefgABCDEFGhijklmnHIJKLMNopqrstuv
abcdefgABCDEFGhijklmnHIJKLMNopqrstuv

Fixed spaces were used for the indent on each line; note how the value changed.

Chapter 13

Typographic Arithmetic

Desktop Typography with QuarkXPress

There are three principal point systems used in the Western world these days; they differ basically in decimal detail:

The American–British System, universally used by English-speaking countries, has for its standard of measurement the .166-inch pica, and the .01383-inch point, which is one-twelfth of the pica. Thus, 1,000 lines of pica or 12-point type set solid measures 166 inches; 1,000 lines of 6-point matter measures 83 inches; and so on.

The Didot System, used in France and most countries of Continental Europe, except Belgium, uses the cicero as its basic unit. The cicero equals 12 "corps" or .178", and the Didot "corps" or point measures exactly .01483".

The Mediaan System, used principally in Belgium, has a "corps" or point measurement of .01374". The Mediaan em or cicero measures .165 of an inch.

For general or practical measurement purposes, three decimals, or even thousandths of an inch, are deemed sufficient. If the fourth decimal equals five or more in this instance, the third is then increased by one.

The first point system was born when Tolbert Lanston invented the Monotype. He wanted to separate the functions of input and output and needed a method that would let the input operator know when to end a line for justification. Arithmetic was the best idea: he would add up character widths. To store the widths of every character in *every* point size of *every* face would have been prohibitive. So he created *relative* widths.

In any typeface all characters are proportional to one another. The proportionality remains the same regardless of point size. Thus, if you describe the width of every character as a multiple of a constant value (unit), the numerical relationships between the characters will remain unchanged no matter what the size is.

An "a" in 9 point might be 8/100ths of a unit; the "a" in 72 point is also 8/100ths of a unit. You differentiate the real width that these characters occupy by multiplying the relative values by the point size:

9-point x 8 unit "a" = 72
72-point x 8 unit "a" = 576

Point systems

The unit system

Desktop Typography with QuarkXPress

Thus, one set of values applies to all sizes of a particular typeface. Lanston's base was 18 and that served phototypesetting for many years. In order to speed up font manufacture, suppliers moved to 36-, 54- and 72-unit systems. Newer laser printers use a 1000-unit system. All letterspacing is performed in increments of the unit system. QuarkXPress, for example uses 1/200 of an em space as the basic unit for negative and positive letterspacing.

Alphabet length

The length of a typed alphabet can also serve as a basic unit. The alphabet used in the examples below is the lowercase *a* through *z*. By comparing the length of these letters (when set normally in the same size) for different typefaces, you can evaluate comparative "mass." A typeface with a relatively short alphabet length would set more characters in a given space than a typeface with a longer alphabet length. The relationship between characters and picas is also expressed as "characters per pica" (CPP)—the number of characters that fit in one pica.

abcdefghijklmnopqrstuvwxyz
abcdefghijklmnopqrstuvwxyz
abcdefghijklmnopqrstuvwxyz
abcdefghijklmnopqrstuvwxyz
abcdefghijklmnopqrstuvwxyz
abcdefghijklmnopqrstuvwxyz
abcdefghijklmnopqrstuvwxyz
abcdefghijklmnopqrstuvwxyz
abcdefghijklmnopqrstuvwxyz

All of the type styles above are set in the same point size. Note that the design of their letters causes the disproportion in apparent mass.

Character count

The character count of a document is the average number of characters per line multiplied by the total lines.

Characters Per Line = CPP × Line Length

To arrive at a character count for a line of typed material, count the number of characters in an inch (even better, average the counts of a couple of inches). Measure the width of the line of type and multiply this figure by the number of characters per inch. The product is (approximately) the number of characters on the line The *pica* typewriter has large characters (10 per inch); the *elite* typewriter has smaller characters (12 per inch).

`Pica at 12 characters per inch`

To establish a character count for a document, figure the number of characters per line using the method in the preceding paragraph. Count the number of lines on a page and multiply this figure by the number of pages. The result is the number of lines in the document. Multiply this figure by the number of characters per line.

You can use this kind of figuring to determine the optimum point size for a given document. For example: if, by your character figuring, your document is going to to be 22 pages long set in 12-point type with 12-point leading and you want to fit it into 20 pages, reduce the point size a point or two.

Copyfitting charts are helpful when you have to figure point sizes for documents. By establishing accurate character counts for a typeface, it is easy to determine what effect increasing or decreasing point size will have on the overall length of a document. For example, if 10-point type will result in a document that only fits 80 percent of the size you want to fill, you can increase the point size by about 20 percent to fill the remaining space.

 This kind of figuring is now archaic, since form and content merge within the desktop world. A manuscript created with a word processing program can be imported into QuarkXPress and formatted typographically to arrive at an accurate page or line count. A variety of tracking, scaling, and leading options allows you to manipulate text to fill space.

Sizing type to fit space with QuarkXPress

Desktop Typography with QuarkXPress

The chart below shows how many lines of a certain point size
will fit into a given column depth. For example, there are 12
lines of 6-point type in 1 inch.

	Type Size in Points											
Column Inch	6	7	8	9	10	11	12	13	14	15	16	18
1/4	3	2	2	2	1	1	1	1	1	1	1	1
1/2	6	5	4	4	3	3	3	2	2	2	2	2
3/4	9	7	6	6	5	4	4	4	3	3	3	3
1	12	10	9	8	7	6	6	5	5	4	4	4
2	24	20	18	16	14	13	12	11	10	9	9	8
3	36	30	27	24	21	19	18	16	15	14	13	12
4	48	41	36	32	28	26	24	22	20	19	18	16
5	60	51	45	40	36	32	30	27	25	24	22	20
6	72	61	54	48	43	39	36	33	30	28	27	24
7	84	72	63	56	50	45	42	38	36	33	31	28
8	96	82	72	64	57	52	48	44	41	38	36	32
9	108	92	81	72	64	58	54	49	46	43	40	36
10	120	102	90	80	72	65	60	55	51	48	45	40
11	132	113	99	88	79	71	66	60	56	52	49	44
12	144	123	108	96	86	78	72	66	61	57	54	48
13	156	133	117	104	93	84	78	71	66	62	58	52
14	168	144	126	112	100	91	84	77	72	67	63	56
15	180	154	135	120	108	97	90	82	77	72	67	60
16	192	164	144	128	115	104	96	88	82	76	72	64
17	204	174	153	136	122	110	102	93	87	81	76	68
18	216	185	162	144	129	116	108	99	92	86	81	72
19	228	195	171	152	136	123	114	105	97	91	85	76
20	240	205	180	160	144	130	120	110	102	96	90	80
21	252	216	189	168	151	136	126	116	108	100	94	84
22	264	226	198	176	158	142	132	121	113	105	99	88
23	276	236	207	184	165	149	138	126	118	109	103	96
24	288	246	216	192	172	156	144	131	123	114	108	99

Desktop Typography with QuarkXPress

The chart below will provide a quick reference to inches, millimeters, points, and picas.

Inch	mm	Points	Picas
.063	1.586	4.517	.376
.078	1.984	5.646	.471
.094	2.381	6.775	.565
.109	2.778	7.904	.659
.125	3.175	9.034	.753
.141	3.572	10.163	.847
.156	3.969	11.292	.941
.172	4.366	12.421	1.035
.188	4.763	13.551	1.129
.203	5.159	14.680	1.223
.219	5.556	15.809	1.317
.234	5.953	16.938	1.412
.250	6.350	18.068	1.506
.266	6.747	19.196	1.599
.281	7.144	20.326	1.694
.297	7.541	21.455	1.788
.313	7.938	22.584	1.882
.328	8.334	23.713	1.976

Desktop Typography with QuarkXPress

QuarkXPress lets you work with a variety of measurements systems: inches, inches (decimal), picas/inches, picas, points, millimeters, or ciceros. (Measurement preferences are set in **Measure** sub-menu in the Preferences dialog box found under the **Style** menu. The following chart will help you convert values from one measurement system to another:

Conversion Factors

mm	×	2.8453	TO GET POINTS
mm	×	.2371	TO GET PICAS
mm	×	.0394	TO GET INCHES
POINTS	×	.3515	TO GET mm
POINTS	×	.08335	TO GET PICAS
POINTS	×	.0138	TO GET INCHES
PICAS	×	4.2175	TO GET mm
PICAS	×	12.0	TO GET POINTS
PICAS	×	.166	TO GET INCHES
INCHES	×	25.4	TO GET mm
INCHES	×	72.27	TO GET POINTS
INCHES	×	6.0225	TO GET PICAS

Desktop Typography with QuarkXPress

Chapter 14

Proofing

Desktop Typography with QuarkXPress

There are many good references books for proofing, such as:

Webster's Standard American Style Manual
The Chicago Manual of Style (Prentice-Hall)
The Associated Press Stylebook (Addison Wesley)
The GPO Style Guide (U.S. Government Printing Office)
Words Into Type (Prentice-Hall)
The general-purpose dictionary your organization accepts. (Be careful when using dictionaries to check hyphenation. Believe it or not, there are differences in hyphenation among dictionaries.)

Some additional useful proofing tools:

- Special-purpose dictionaries (medical, electronics, computer science, and so on).
- A type gauge or ruler.

Before proofing a document for details (spelling, punctuation, etc.) you can do a visual check:

- Is the type the right style and size?

- Is the layout correct, and is the copy properly aligned?

- Do the the lines of type in adjoining columns align line for line across the page? You may think unaligned columns are rare, but these days leading controls are often misused to fill white space at the end of a story, especially in newspapers.

- Check line art for clarity and the positions of photographs.

- Check heads and captions for consistency of style. Are all of the main heads set in the same font, style, size, and weight (unless you're deliberately varying them)?

- Are the subheads and captions set consistently?

- Is there a consistent use of caps, uppercase, and mixed case?

- Paragraph indents should be uniform. If there are no indents, there should be additional space between paragraphs to allow a visual pause for the reader.

- Check the leading between lines with a type gauge.

Some tips about proofreading for accuracy: In addition to checking spelling, grammar and punctuation, you should look for:

- In justified composition and in short lines, it's possible to have lines ending with hyphens. These may have been embedded by whoever typed the original text, or more likely they were created by an automatic hyphenation utility. Having hyphenated words end two lines in a row is okay; three lines ending with hyphens is not okay. If this problem comes up, ask the author if a word or two can be changed.

- Remember that humans are fallible when it comes to hyphenating words. Computers are even worse. Even the best hyphenation utilities will make mistakes. Watch out for them. Keep a good dictionary on hand, and beware of the common error of leaving less than two characters before the hyphen.

- Unless your publishing program is a real loser, your word spacing should be even. However, it *can* be too tight, or more often, too wide. You've seen ugly lines that consist of three words, one at either end and one in the middle, and a lot of empty space between. In computer typesetting, this happens when there's no hyphenation routine and the program is justifying lines of type. Manually hyphenate to fix this problem. QuarkXPress uses the Knuth algorithm for hyphenation via rules of logic (algorithm). You can also create your own dictionary of exception words that are always hyphenated according to your instructions.

- **Widows** are short lines ending paragraphs that fall either at the end of a page or column or at the top of a page or column.

- **Orphans** are single lines that have spilled over to the top of a page or column. Widows and orphans should be reunited with at least a couple of lines of copy. Remedies include adjusting the word or character spacing, or asking the author to rewrite the paragraph.

- Programs without hyphenation routines will first try to justify a line by adding spaces between words until a limit is reached. After that, space is added between characters. You can solve the word space problem by setting a low limit; however, you may end up with odd-looking, stretched words. This can usually be fixed by hyphenating a word.

- To be on the safe side, make sure lines of type align along the baseline. A glitch in the printing device can cause an irregular line. This is especially true with laser printers, in which the paper can drag or catch when feeding.

- Blacks should be dense black. Whites should be clean. Characters shouldn't be broken or scratched. Watch out with laser printers. The density can vary across the page.

- It's easy for someone who is typing to omit sentences or even paragraphs, especially with proximate groups of words that begin with the same word or phrase. Almost everyone forgets a word in a sentence every now and then.

The next two pages show the primary proofing symbols that are used to mark copy for revision:

Delete, Take out copy

This mark indicates that material is to be deleted. It is usually assumed that the space that results from the removal is to be closed up. In some cases the proofreader may specifically indicate "close up" by combining the delete mark with the close up marks.

EXAMPLE

Practical Typography

RESULT

Practical Typography

Exclamation point

Also called a "bang" or "screamer". From the Latin "Io" for joy, once written as Io

EXAMPLE

Practical Typography

RESULT

Practical Typography!

Apostrophe

Because this mark looks just like the comma, the v-shape and loop are used to distinguish it.

EXAMPLE

GAMAs Practical Typography

RESULT

GAMA's Practical Typography

Hyphen

May be indicated in any of the above ways.

EXAMPLE

Practical Typography

RESULT

Practical-Typography

Space

This is the shorthand notation for "space"– horizontal or vertical. It is usually used in conjunction with the "insert" mark or an arrow of some type.

EXAMPLE

PracticalTypography

RESULT

Practical Typography

EXAMPLE

Practical Typography
Practical Typography

RESULT

Practical Typography
Practical Typography

EXAMPLE

Practical Typography
Practical Typography
Practical Typography

RESULT

Practical Typography
Practical Typography
Practical Typography

Separate

Two items are too close together and should be separated.

EXAMPLE

Practical Typography

RESULT

Practical Typography

Change to small caps; make small caps

Copy with two lines beneath it is to be in small capitals. Small caps are usually as high as the x-height.

EXAMPLE

GAMA's Practical Typography

RESULT

GAMA's Practical Typography

Line up

Vert.   Horiz.

Copy that is not in alignment is to be corrected as indicated.

EXAMPLE

Practical
Typography

RESULT

Practical
Typography

Brackets

Since these marks are somewhat similar to those for "move over" you must make them distinct so that it is known that they printout.

EXAMPLE

Practical Typography

RESULT

[Practical Typography]

Em Dash (or En Dash)

There is a distinct difference between the mark for a hyphen and a dash. Dashes are usually in EM and EN widths, although some systems make only have a 3/4 EM dash. When multiple dashes are being indicated, make sure that the number is plain.

EXAMPLE

practical typography

RESULT

practical—typography

Multiples are usually used when only the first letter of a word is printed (Mr. B—), especially if profanity is used (Go to h—), or if a statement ends abruptly (The murderer is —).

Dashes of this length are usually used as a rule to separate heads and text, footnotes and text, or other copy. Three dashes are also used where names are repeated in a bibliography or other listing one beneath another.

OR |1| |EN| |2|

Make boldface

The copy indicated with a wavy line beneath it is to be in boldface.

EXAMPLE

Practical Typography b.f.

RESULT

Practical Typography

Space evenly

Insert and equal amount of space at the points indicated.

EXAMPLE

This is Practical Typography

RESULT

This is Practical Typography

Comma

The comma is made as a bold dot with a strong curved line. It must be written distinctly to distinguish it from quotes and is further emphasized by placing a triangular shaped roof over it.

EXAMPLE

Practical Typography a guide

RESULT

Practical Typography, a guide

Superior or Inferior Characters

or ∨ for superior

or ∧ for inferior

EXAMPLE

$a^2 + b^2 = c^2$

RESULT

$a^2 + b^2 = c^2$

EXAMPLE

H_2O

RESULT

H_2O

Period

A dot in a circle indicates a period. The circle is important since the smallness of the dot may cause it to be overlooked. Three of these marks are used to indicate an ellipsis.

EXAMPLE

Practical Typography

RESULT

Practical Typography.

EXAMPLE

Practical Typography

RESULT

Practical Typography . . .

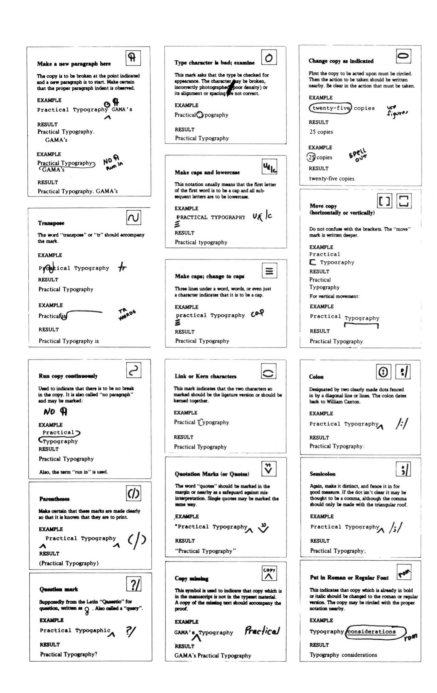

Chapter 15

Applied Typography

The most visible manifestation of point size is the x-height of the characters in a font. The x-height is simply the height of the letter "x"—representing the most important area of the letterform for 90 percent of the lowercase characters:

X-height

The x-height is a more realistic measurement of the size of a typeface than point size, and it is reflected in the size of all of the other characters as well.

Look at the following examples:

XxXXXXXx

HHHHHHHH

All of the type in the two lines above is 24-point, yet it is evident that the x's and H's are different sizes. The differences are a combination of:

- type style
- type size
- leading
- column width
- intercharacter spacing

All of these factors determine the overall "color" of a typographic page.

The color of a page of type refers to the overall shade of gray perceived by your eye. The gray mass can be interrupted by poor word or character spacing or uneven leading. Manipulating typographic color can only be accomplished by reviewing type after setting and adjusting the variables.

Typographic color

Rivers are patterns of white running down the page that result from the random position of word spaces in adjacent lines. Again, you must review type after it has been set to find and correct the problem of distracting rivers.

Other problems you should be aware of:

- Word spacing (it should be consistent)
- Widowed lines (eliminate wherever possible)
- Poor letterspacing (use kerning where needed)
- Uneven right margin caused by too many hyphens in a

row (reset)

- A general, even, consistent appearance (including the density or "blackness " of the type).

Contour

When you modify a margin to create an irregularly shaped edge, it is called a contour or run-around. Run-arounds are accomplished by using varying line indents. A special sheet with pica and point gradations is used to calculate the value of the indents. The sheet is usually transparent and placed over the art or shape so that all indents can be established. Newer systems allow you to indicate the shape via mouse or palette and then automatically establish the indents for the contour.

With QuarkXPress, you can use the rectangle, rounded corner, and oval picture box tools to create shapes that you want type to run-around. The type automatically runs around the shapes you create. The semi-circular run-around in the preceding paragraph was created using the oval picture box tool.

Contrast

Typography is based on symmetry, a predictable pattern or arrangement. Symmetry is order and balance—all elements in harmony. Asymmetry is the opposite, with no predictable pattern. Contrast is a form of asymmetry. It is essentially, a *difference* between items. In typography, we deal with contrasts in:

1. Size
   NNNNNNNNNNNNN

2. Weight
   NNNNNNNNNNNN

3. Width
   NNNNNNNNNNNNNN

4. Form
   NNNNNNNNNNN

5. Structure
   NNNNNNNNNNNNN

6. Placement
   NNNNNNNN^NNNNNN

7. Posture
NNNNNNN*NNNNNN*

…and combinations of the above items.

Digital type gets its name from digital computers, which are based on the binary principle of ON/OFF. A digital image is created with dots; the individual dot is either there or not there—on or off.

Digital type

The individual dot is called a *pel* or *pixel* (both terms are short for "picture element"), and a group of overlapping dots forming a straight or curved line is called a *raster*.

Typesetters who use line segments or "vectors" to outline a character still use dots as the basic building blocks.

Because every character is made up of dots, the edges of diagonals and curves may not be as smooth and sharp as straight lines. At 1000 dots per inch (a measurement of resolution), acceptable resolution quality is produced.

The best items to check when determining quality levels is the dot on the lowercase i and the entire Optima typeface:

●

Since digital type exists in memory or "program" form, it may be manipulated electronically to produce:

1. More point size increments. QuarkXPress allows you to set type size in quarter of a point increments.
2. Oblique or backslant characters. Permissible for use with sans serif type only.
3. Expanded and condensed characters.
4. Reverse type (white on black).
5. Outlines, drop shadows, shaded type, and other special effects.

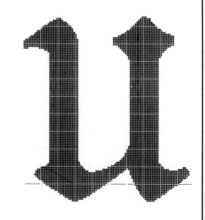

A bit map defines each dot position

Desktop Typography with QuarkXPress

Formats

A format is any combination of point size, line spacing (leading), line length, typeface, placement, and style that contributes to producing a specific typographic appearance on a page. Formatting may relate to a character, word, line, paragraph, section, page, group of pages, or an entire publication.

Formats can be expressed by specifying each of the items in the preceding paragraph. With computers, there is a quicker method: storing the format information and referencing with a keyboard command.

 With QuarkXPress you can create customized style sheets for your documents. You can prespecify font, size, color (if you have a color monitor) shade, style (bold, italic, underline, etc.) horizontal scale, and tracking for various typographic elements—heads, body copy, photo cutlines, and such. You can establish keyboard equivalents for your style sheets, which allow you to change styles easily without having to use the menu.

Galley

Galley refers to a long piece of typeset material, a take. In hot metal, a metal tray with raised edges held about 20 inches of metal type. Thus, jobs were broken down into workable units for proofing and handling.

The term came to refer both to the length of material and its state. Since a galley proof was made right after type was set, it was a "first" or "reading" proof. Subsequently, the material would be corrected and organized into pages to create "final," "page," or "repro" proofs.

Thus, a galley is a rough proof or copy of a length of typeset material in an intermediate state—somewhere between the original and the final, camera-ready page. Today, galleys are not usually of equal lengths when output from a phototypesetter; they are equal-sized when output from a page printer.

Gutters and margins

Gutters are the spaces between columns of type. Gutter width is usually determined by the number and width of columns and the overall width of the area to be filled. Sometimes a rule is used in addition to blank space.

Gutters should not be so narrow that columns appear to run together. When narrow gutters are required, a rule line is often used.

Margins are the borders around the outside edges of a page.

Initial letters that are different from the type of the text are some-times used at the beginning of chapters and paragraphs.

Initial letters

The most common style, and the oldest, is the sunken or "drop cap" position. In this case, the initial letter is larger than the accompanying text and is dropped below the first line of the copy. It does not rise above the top line of the text.

Another style is the raised or "stick up" initial letter. It rests on the baseline of the first or subsequent line of text and rises above the top line.

The most important consideration when using initial letters is *fit*. Be aware of the following:

1. Square or contoured format
2. Left margin should be aligned or indented
3. Left margin aligned or optically aligned
4. Cap, small-cap, or lowercase lead-in
5. Related or non-related type style

The space around the initial letter should be the same on the side as it is on the bottom.

In all cases the letter must align at the base of a line of text.

A raised initial letter must also rest on the baseline, and kern-ing should be done where necessary.

Raised letters may also be indented from the margin.

"If quotes are to be set, they should be in the cap size. You can also set them in a size between the text and the initial letter size.

The initial cap may rest on the baseline and rise above the text (as illustrated above). This is done with a simple point size change. Traditionally, the first word following the initial was set in small caps or capitals.

Also note that type should contour the initial cap. For example, if the first word of a paragraph begins with a raised cap T, the subsequent letters should be kerned to fall below the arm of the T.

N othing works better than a
square-shaped initial cap.

Stick up or raised initial

The raised initial cap N in the illustration above is one of the most common styles, mainly because it is very easy to accomplish. Simply change the point size of the first letter. The example is 10-point text with an 18-point initial. A relationship of about 2:1 is best. The example is also easy because the initial cap is a square character. However, sometimes fate is not kind and you get:

T his kind of initial cap
can cause problems

 The preceding example is a typographer's worst nightmare. The solution is simple if you have the right tools. With QuarkXPress, you first create your initial raised letter; then place the insertion point between the initial and the first letter of text and select the **Kern** menu command under the **Style** menu. Enter a negative value to close up the space between the initial and the first letter of text. A -3 value was used for the example below:

T his initial cap was
kerned for appearance.

You can also use some other tricks to make stick up initials work better. One way is to put the rest of the first word (lead-in) in CAPS or SMALL CAPS:

T HIS block of copy is
absolutely meaningless.

This technique relates the initial and the first word more closely to form a cohesive design unit.

Desktop Typography with QuarkXPress

Typographic license, used with taste, can yield an endless variety of visually appealing combinations, such as:

T<small>HIS</small> is a style of initial

In the example above, a 24-point letter in a sans serif bold typeface was used for the initial capital. Or:

T<small>HIS</small> block of copy
is absolutely meaningless

Here, the first line is indented several en spaces to let white space help define the initial area.

T<small>HIS</small> block of copy is an example of another style of initial cap — the drop cap. This block of copy is an example of another style of initial cap — the drop cap.

Raised caps are a piece of cake; drop caps can be tricky. With QuarkXPress, drop caps can be created quickly and easily. Simple draw a text box that will contain the initial letter. Make the letter the size and style you want, and use the handles on the text box to pull the edges as close as you want to the initial. If you want to contour the text to wrap around the initial, make the box transparent using the **Modify** menu command under the **Item** menu; use the space bar to position the text where you want it relative to your initial.

Technically and typographically, the baseline of the sunken initial should align with the baseline of one of the text lines. That is Rule 1. Rule 2 is that the space on the right of the initial letter must be optically equal to the leading value in use. Thus, the initial floats in its area.

If the initial letter is square, it simply floats in a rectangular box, with the text aligning at the right edge. However, when the letter is diagonal or oval, you must kern to move the first letter of text closer to the edge of the initial.

Drop caps

T his paragraph is an example of what can be done with odd-shaped letters using QuarkXPress. The 50-point initial was set in a separate text box. The box was made transparent using the **Modify** menu command under the **Edit** menu. A combination of hard returns at the right ends and spaces at the left ends of the first three lines was used to create the "wrap."

Typing or setting text lines to the same length so that they line up on the left *and* the right margins is called justification. The practice originated with medieval scribes who ruled margins and text lines to speed their writing and to fit as many characters on a line as possible. They also thought it looked nice.

Later, metal type required *even* copy blocks to allow "lock up" into page form. So, there are three historical reasons behind justified type: the scribes' quest for speed and their need to conserve paper; the requirements of technology; and aesthetics. Why do we justify lines? Who knows? It is now traditional and one of the hallmarks of professional typography.

Justification

Justification is accomplished by putting as much type on a line as possible until the last possible word or syllable fits and then dividing the remaining white space among the word spaces on the line. This is why word spaces are variable in width in justified text. The spaces are expanded or contracted as needed to fill the line out to its justification width.

Margins are the imaginary vertical demarcations for text or tabular columns. Overall or primary margins are established by the line length function or the cumulative total of secondary margins (tab or text columns).

A conventional page of type is rectangular, with left and right column margins parallel to the edges of the page. To make a line of type, regardless of the words in it, exactly the same length as its fellow lines is to *justify* the line. This is still common practice in bookmaking (less so in advertising material), and many word processors are equipped to justify lines as well.

Bricks are uniformly sized; words aren't. Since words can't be hyphenated indiscriminately (they must be hyphenated between syllables), the spacing between words in justified lines of type are not exactly the same in each line.

As lines become shorter, the problem with white space becomes more acute. In an index, for example, when an entry runs for two or more lines, the runover lines must be indented under the first line, thus making the runover line even shorter. Sometimes there is room for only two medium-sized words on a line, with enough space between them to accommodate another, shorter, word because the next word in the entry is too long to fit on the line and cannot be divided (*through* or *passed*, for example).

Lines of type that are not justified are ragged. Ragged right is the most common style of "rag" type. It is used occasionally in magazines, newspapers, and advertising.

What's the preferred style of type? Justified or rag? The debate will go on forever. Justified type gives a formal look to copy; ragged right is more informal. Most research shows that rag-right type is slightly more legible. Researchers list possible reasons:

Ragged vs. justified

- The spacing between words and letters is consistent from line to line. This is also possible with sophisticated hyphenation and justification routines producing justified copy.
- The eye tracks more easily from the end of different length lines back to the beginning of the next line.

Choose rag right if you're using a sans serif typeface. The squarish letterforms of sans serif fonts coupled with squared-off lines makes justified sans serif harder to read. Use rag right for short copy blocks.

If you turn a typeset page upside down and the word spaces are clearly visible, the word spacing is too wide. In high-quality typesetting, systems control letterspacing carefully. Certain letter pairs, particularly capital letter pairs (such as W A), appear to be improperly letterspaced when typeset normally. By kerning letters—carefully adjusting the letterspacing—type can be controlled to be more aesthetically pleasing.

Paragraphs are units of English composition—copy blocks. Paragraphs are defined by an indent at the beginning of the first line and often delineated by a short line of characters at the end. (Indents should be at least one em; slightly larger is preferred.)

Paragraphs

An alternative method of distinguishing paragraphs is to increase the line spacing between them. You can also run paragraphs together and separate them by using a special symbol, such as the paragraph symbol (¶). For this book paragraphs are defined with extra line space.

Proper justification sometimes involves breaking the last word in a line (because only part of it will fit) into two pieces so that word spacing remains consistent. Of course, proper justification must also be done according to hyphenation rules; words must be broken between syllables.

Like rag copy, word spacing in justified copy should be as consistent as possible. Also, no more than three hyphens in a row (some say two) should appear at the ends of lines.

Widows and orphans

A short line at the end of a paragraph that is less than one-third the line length is called a "widow." Sometimes a widow is defined as the carryover letters of a hyphenated word (if there are no other characters on the line). A widow that occurs at the top of a column or page is called an "orphan." Widows and orphans should be avoided if possible. There are only a few ways of getting rid of them:

1. Rewrite the copy
2. Increase the word space size to wrap more copy
3. Use negative letterspacing (tracking) to tighten copy
4. Use positive letterspacing (tracking) to open up copy

In regard to ragged copy, there is continuing argument about how ragged ragged should be and whether or not hyphenation should be allowed. Traditionally, ragged meant that the words fell where they fell—no hyphenation, uniform word spacing. Today there is a school of thought that says hyphenation and variable word spacing are permissible to make the rag of ragged copy look "light." Be careful when hyphenating ragged copy; a light rag can look like bad justification.

There are no rules carved in concrete—only those you or someone else makes.

Unlike a typewriter, which creates word spaces of the same width, the word space in typography is *variable*—it expands or contracts depending on the length of the line, the number of characters on the line, and the number of word spaces on the line.

Here's an important piece of information to keep in mind: the justification process can only work with *variable* word spaces. People who work with justified type must realize that a word space cannot be used as an indent or in other places where a *fixed* constant width space is required.

Word spaces are controlled by prespecifying minimum, optimum, and maximum widths. These variables can be tailored by users according to their own taste.

The *minimum* word space is the smallest value (size) allowed. A properly set minimum value ensures that word spacing will be visually attractive no matter how much words are forced together in the justification processes.

The *maximum* word space is the widest value allowed, and usually this is the threshold point at which automatic letterspacing might be employed (if allowable).

The *optimum* word space is the size that produces the best spacing (this value is roughly equal to the width of the lowercase i of the font and size being used).

In ragged type and quadded lines, the optimum word space value is usually used throughout.

Tabs

Setting tabs—it's one of the most difficult aspects of typography. In the days of hot metal type and later with phototypesetting, tabular material was created using fixed widths: the en space was the same width as the figures and the Thin space was the same width as the punctuation. They were multiples of one another so that copy could be aligned against defined margins.
There was no such thing as automatic decimal alignment.

Setting tabs with QuarkXPress

With QuarkXPress, the **Tabs** menu command is under the **Style** menu. When selected, it brings up a dialog box that allows you to define an exact tab point (to 1/1000th of a unit). You can create left, right, center, and decimal tabs; you can also set fill characters (leaders) for any tab.

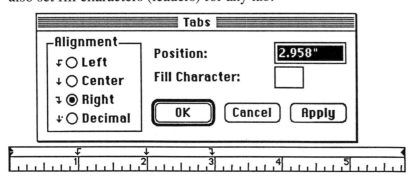

Tabs Dialog Box

Chapter 16

Hyphenation

Hyphenation essentially prevents the word spaces from being stretched or compressed to a visually disturbing point. When the system detects that the word spaces are getting too big, the first word of the next line is pulled back and the program inserts a hyphen between syllables. The opposite happens when the spaces are too narrow and part of the last word is pushed to the next line. The difficulty of automated hyphenation is that you need a program that encompasses all the rules and exceptions for hyphenation in the English (or any other) language.

Hyphenation

The basic rules for hyphenation are:

Hyphenation rules

- There must be at least two characters on either side of the hyphen point. Three is optimum.
- Numerals should not be hyphenated (but they could be in an "emergency" at a comma point).
- It is not good practice to hyphenate in a headline.
- Never hyphenate a one-syllable word.
- Divide on a double consonant, unless the word root ends with a double consonant (e.g. "miss-ing," "rent-al").
- Not more than three hyphens in a row at the ends of lines are allowable.

An incorrect word division is called a "bad break."

- Hyphenation at the end of a line should occur at the proper syllable breaks.
- There should be no more than three hyphenated line endings in a row.
- Hyphenate between two consonants when they are pronounced separately.
- Divide compound words between the elemental words, such as proofreading—proof-reading.
- Divide hyphenated compound words on the compounding hyphen.
- If the first vowel in the word is short, divide after the consonant that follows it.
- Double consonants may be divided after part of the original word.
- Hyphenate to maintain syllabic endings.
- Divide between vowels when each is pronounced separately.
- When the first vowel is long, divide after the vowel.

Dividing words at syllables

- Hyphenate after definite prefixes if it doesn't change pronunciation.
- Hyphenate before a definite suffix if it doesn't change pronunciation.

Try to avoid hyphenation (or simply breaking lines) in the following cases:

- Words of fewer than six letters
- One syllable words—*never* hyphenate
- Instances in which a syllable of fewer than two characters will be carried over (it's okay, however, to leave such a syllable at the end of a line and carry the rest of the word to the next line)
- Words with two syllables pronounced as one
- Quantities, amounts, and figures—but there can be exceptions
- Proper nouns, such as a person's name
- Abbreviations
- Right after references such as A) or 1)
- Between a person's first and middle names or between initials (although the surname may be carried to the next line if necessary)
- Right before or after abbreviated titles such as Mr., Ms., Dr., and Sr.

Do not feel compelled to hyphenate just because the opportunity is there to do it. Hyphenation is only a means to avoid large gaps between words. The objective of good typesetting is to get an overall gray appearance without rivers of white. Some word gaps are more acceptable than setting more than three justified lines to end with some kind of punctuation (this includes periods and commas, as well as hyphens). Bookstores carry several good dictionaries on correct word hyphenation. Foreign dictionaries will help you hyphenate non-English words.

Rules of logic

Some typical rules of logic used by computers in regard to hyphenation follow (but there are many exceptions):

- Insert a hyphen before the suffixes -ing, -ed, -ly, -ty, and -day.
- Insert a hyphen after the prefixes non-, pop-, air-, mul-, gas-, gar-, cor-, con-, com-, dis-, ger-, out-, pan-, psy-, syn-, sur-, sul-, suf-, sub-, mis-, ul-, un-, im-, il-, ig-, eu-, es-, os-, and up-.

- Insert a hyphen in a sequence of numbers broken up by commas after a comma.
- Do not hyphenate if less than five letters in a word, or if less than two characters before or after a hyphen. For example: open, not o-pen.
- Do not insert a hyphen before the suffix -ing if preceded by one of the letters d, t, or h.
- Do not insert a hyphen before the suffix -ed if preceded by one of the letters v, r, t, p.
- Do not insert a hyphen before the suffix -ly if the word ends in bly.
- Do not insert a hyphen before the suffix -ty if the word ends in hty.

Other general rules are:

Breaking words correctly

- Know the author's meaning of words that are spelled alike but have different meanings. They are hyphenated differently, for example, de-sert and des-ert or min-ute and mi-nute.
- Proper names may be divided. Since they are not generally found in hyphenation dictionaries, however, you will have to rely on good sense.
- Don't divide a one-syllable word or the added suffix from a one-syllable base word.
- Don't divide a word so that only one letter is left at the beginning or ending of a line.
- *Never* hyphenate a word if it means you will have a widow on the next line.
- Use *"20,000 Words"* for word divisions unless otherwise instructed.
- A word may be divided *only* at the end of a syllable.
- Words pronounced as one syllable should never be divided, such as crashed, drowned, through, and down.
- Words of two syllables in which one is a single vowel should not be divided, for example, around, even, over and efficient.
- A terminating syllable of only two letters should not be carried over unless absolutely necessary in a very narrow measure.
- A division before a single vowel that alone forms a syllable should be avoided except in the case of the suffixes -able and -ible (con-sid-er-able and dis-cern-ible) and words in which the vowel is the first syllable of a root. For example munici-pal is preferred over mu-nic-ipal; privi-lege not priv-ilege.

Desktop Typography with QuarkXPress

- When the final consonant of a verb is doubled in forming the past tense or the participle, the second consonant belongs with the letters following. Single or double consonants at the end of the root word should not be carried over. For example, occur-ring, forget-ting, forc-ing, and install-ing.
- Abbreviations such as M.A., Ph.D., YMCA, A.M., etc., should not be divided nor should space be inserted between letters.
- Do not put the initials of a name on different lines and avoid separating initials, titles, and degrees from a name. If proper nouns must be broken, use rules of hyphenation.
- Avoid dividing at the ends of more than two successive lines.
- Do not divide the last word of a paragraph. This creates a widow.
- Avoid dividing the last word on a right-hand page. This creates an orphan on the next page.
- Avoid dividing a hyphenated compound word except at the hyphen. For example, mother-/in-/law and up-/to-/date.
- Avoid dividing combinations like 98.6F, 14 B.C., 6:30 P.M.
- Avoid separating (a) or (1) from the matter to which it pertains.
- Do not separate the day from the month. The year may be on the next line.
- If necessary, a number of five numerals or more may be divided at the end of a line, using a hyphen as in a word. The division should always be made at a comma, and the comma should be retained before the hyphen.

Homographs

Homographs are those annoying words that are spelled the same but pronounced differently. Thus, their hyphenation depends upon their meaning. Here is a list of the more common homographs:

as-so-ciate	as-so-ci-ate	*bus-ses*	buss-es
chart-er	char-ter	*de-sert*	des-ert
for-mer	form-er	*in-val-id*	in-va-lid
lus-ter	lust-er	*min-ute*	mi-nute
pla-ner	plan-er	*pre-ce-dent*	prec-e-dent
pre-sent	pres-ent	*pro-ject*	proj-ect
prod-uce	pro-duce	*prog-ress*	pro-gress
reb-el	re-bel	*re-cord*	rec-ord
ref-use	re-fuse	*re-sume*	re-su-me

Desktop Typography with QuarkXPress

With QuarkXPress hyphenation is controlled in two ways:

    1. Algorithmic hyphenation based upon Knuth
    2. Exception dictionary hyphenation

H & J with QuarkXPress

You can add words to the Exception Dictionary indicating the desired hyphenation. You can also test how the program would hyphenate a word by using the **Suggested Hyphenation** function under the **Utilities** menu. This function shows the hyphen points for any word to the left of the insert bar.

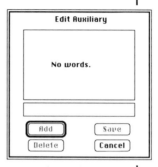

The **H&J** function under the **Preferences** menu lets you specify the "maximum hyphens in a row" in order to preserve letter/word space consistency. You can also define allowable hyphens in a row, characters before and after the hyphen point, and word space values.

Chapter 17

Books

Desktop Typography with QuarkXPress

Book arrangement

This chapter is provided not so much because books are primary publications of publishing systems, but because the underlying principles for the formatting and design of books are basic to almost all other types of print communication. The arrangement of the various parts of a book has been more or less standardized by custom, even though some of the parts may be missing in a given publication.

The following terms refer to the setting of pages for books:

Verso: the left page.
Recto: the right page.
Folio : the page number.
Running head and **running foot:** the book name (usually) appearing on every page, top or bottom.
Chapter opening: the first page of a chapter, usually a recto page.
Line short and **line long:** the allowance for setting certain pages one line longer or shorter than page depth to eliminate widows or short pages, or to make allowance for illustrations or tables.
Widow: a last line of a paragraph that is less than one third the full width of the line, usually the carryover of a hyphenated word.
Orphan: a widow that falls at the top of a column or page.

Front Matter:

Half Title: book title alone on page.
Fact Title: list of other books by the book's author (faces title page).
Title Page: always a right hand (recto) page.
Copyright: must be on title page or, more commonly, on the reverse.
Dedication: may be on copyright page; usually a recto page; usually alone on page.
Introduction: Always recto.
Preface: same as Foreword, Introduction.
Acknowledgement, Contents: always recto.
List of Illustrations, List of Figures: Maps, Charts, Tables.
Introduction: Always recto.

Front matter pages are numbered with Roman numerals, i thru xvii, for example, in lowercase.

Back Matter:

Appendix: Notes, quotations, bibliography.
Glossary:
Index:
Colophon: Provides production details.

Page forms

- A sheet of paper printed as one page is a *broadside*.
- Fold it once and it is a *folio* (4 pages).
- Fold it twice and it is a *quarto* (8 pages).
- Fold it three times and it is a *octavo* (16 pages).
- Fold it four times and it is a *16 mo* (32 pages).
- Fold it five times and it is a *32 mo* (64 pages).

Colophons

The first colophon appears in Fust and Schoeffer's Psalter of 1457. A colophon describes certain production information about the book, most often about the typography.

Fust and Schoeffer's Psalter of 1457

Pagination

All modern books are paginated consecutively, and all leaves in a book (except end papers) are counted in the pagination, whether page-numbered folios are used or not. A folio can be placed in a variety of positions on a page. The most common and perhaps the most easily found place is at the top of the page, flush with the outside margin (left on verso pages, right on recto pages). A folio may also be printed at the bottom of a page. When placed in this location it is called a *drop folio*. Drop folios may be placed flush outside, indented from the outside, or centered.

The preliminary pages of a book, especially books produced in the United States, are usually paginated with lowercase roman numerals. The practice is due partly to tradition and partly to expedience; some of these pages (those containing the table of contents and the lists of illustrations and tables) cannot be finally made up until the text is in page proofs, and others (those containing the preface, acknowledgments, and dedication) are often heavily revised or even added by the author at the last moment, after the rest of the book has already been paginated.

This is not the only system, however. In some books, Arabic numbering begins on the first page (half title) and continues straight through the book. This system, more common in Great Britain than the United States, should be kept in mind as a sometimes useful alternative to the better-known system.

When front matter is unusually long, the use of Arabic numerals eliminates the awkwardness of Roman folios becoming as large as xlviii, xlix, etc. But because this system of Arabic numbering determines the pagination of the entire book, the author must understand that there is no possibility of adding a dedication page or an additional page of acknowledgments once paging has begun.

Whether Roman or Arabic folios are used, no folios are used on display pages (half title, title, copyright, dedication, epigraph), and drop folios (or none) are used on the opening page of each of the subsequent sections of the prelims.

The creation of a book involves page design, typographic considerations (font, size, leading), stylistic considerations (folios or not, use of special characters), and production considerations (type of paper, type of press). The overriding concern regarding book design and layout, as is the case with most publications, is legibility.

The choice of size and paper in the production of a book has a great deal to do with the overall cost of production. Cost considerations can place some restrictions on the physical size of a book. Some of the more common book sizes are 9×12 inches, 6×9 inches, $5\frac{1}{2} \times 8\frac{1}{2}$ inches, and $8\frac{1}{2} \times 11$ inches. Other sizes can be created, but you can expect to pay higher manufacturing costs for a page size that cannot be cut out of a large sheet size.

Though there are no hard and fast rules for page margins in book design, one of the traditional guidelines is to use ratios of 2:3, which means that a page size of 6×9 inches would have an image area of 4×6 inches.

When small type is used for footnotes, the notes may be put in half measure or full measure lines. The space between the two columns when half measure lines are used should not be wider

Footnotes

than the em space of the type used for the footnote and may be even narrower. Half-measure footnotes save space and present a neater appearance than those formed with the straggling lines of the full measure. Frequently white space produced by short lines results from full-measure footnotes.

Setting footnotes in half measure may result in an uneven number of lines in the two parallel columns, but the area of leftover white space at the end (sometimes nine tenths of the broad measure) is not as offensive in the half measure.

The use of half measure for footnotes gives them a distinction that they do not have when set in a broad measure, and it differentiates them from the extracts in a much clearer manner. This method gives a neater appearance to the page, especially when the notes are primarily made up of short citations.

[1] Note 1 is distinct because it stands apart in its own column, and does not appear to be part of note 2.

[2] Note 2 is distinct because it stands apart in its own column, and does not appear to be part of note 1.

Half-measure notes

Half measure should not be used for long lines of poetry, nor for the only note on a page when that note comprises only two nearly full lines. Three lines will justify the use of half measure.

When long lines of verse are put in a footnote, it is injudicious to break these lines in the middle to accommodate them to the half measure. In this instance it is preferable to use the broad measure, but you should use the half measure if it won't result in broken lines.

Sidenotes

Sidenotes are not used as much as they were 50 years ago. The widths most often selected are one broad quotation and two narrow quotations. The size of explanatory sidenotes is seldom larger than six-point.

Setting sidenotes in italic lowercase is not a good idea because slanted letters contrast badly with the upright arabic figures that have to be used to specify dates, pages, and years. When possible, use roman for sidenotes.

This is a cut-in or inset Cut-in or inset notes, more troublesome than sidenotes, are usually set in roman lowercase at least three sizes smaller than the size of the text. Cut-ins take up less space than subheadings. When set with a broad and clearly defined white space around them, insets are distinct enough to attract attention (usually the attention of a student, since insets are often used in textbooks). A small square of white space in the text is an unusual form that attracts attention, but it does not offend the eye, as is often the case with bold type, which spots the page like a blot of ink.

When in doubt, put all the notes at the end of the book and be done with them.

Chapter 18

Anatomy of a Page

Desktop Typography with QuarkXPress

Typography is applied to a broad range of printed material. The following are the most common categories:

Print communication

Ad/Direct Mail

Characterized by heavy use of illustration and color, with a wide variety of type styles. Image area is usually restricted to a single space—such as a page or a portion of a page. Highly layout driven. Self-mailers, for example, are pieces that fold into mailable units.

Flier/Folder

No identifiable typographic pattern. Usually a flat, single sheet of paper or a folded sheet. This category also includes multiple folded sheets collated into sets but not bound.

Brochure/Booklet

Usually multiple folded sheets of paper (less than 32 pages) collated into sets and stapled through the fold (saddle stitched).

Newsletter

Come in a variety of formats:

> Multiple sheets—no binding (3% percent)
> Flyer/Folder (61 percent)
> Brochure/Booklet (36 percent)

Newsletters are the second most popular form of office publishing.

Magazine/Journal

Essentially the same physical format as the brochure/booklet, but usually consisting of more pages. Typographically more consistent than a brochure/booklet. Published on a regular basis.

Newspaper

Either broadsheet or tabloid (half a broadsheet) in size, printed and folded in one pass through the printing press. Has lots of inserts and ink that comes off on your hands.

Book/Manual

Characterized by a high page count and relatively consistent typographic format. Also includes reports, the most popular form of office publishing. Binding is usually adhesive (perfect binding) or sewn, although mechanical binding is also used. Technical manuals and proposals are in this category, as are larger catalogs and directories.

Desktop Typography with QuarkXPress

Print communication

Form/Coupon

Fill-in forms are characterized by heavy use of horizontal and vertical rule lines. Highly erratic formats.

Lists

Includes price lists and product lists, directories, and even catalogs to some extent. Most often single sheets organized into a set, although the sheets could be bound as a directory.

Sign/Poster

Display-oriented material which is usually characterized by large type sizes.

Invitation/Menu

Most often single sheets—fractions of a page—with a moderate number of lines.

Business Card/Letterhead

Limited typography and graphics but highly variable formats.

Envelope/Packaging

Usually small areas of type and limited graphics. Includes tags, labels, covers, jackets, boxes, and wrappers.

Presentations

Include 35mm slides, overhead transparencies, posters, and accompanying hard copy.

Desktop Typography with QuarkXPress

Each of these units has unique characteristics:

	PAGE COUNT	TYPOGRAPHIC VARIABILITY	COLOR USE	BINDING	ILLUSTRATION GRAPHICS USE	PRINT/ COPY
Ad/Direct Mail	Low	High	High	None	High	Print
Flyer/Folder	Low	High	Moderate	Flat/Fold	Moderate	Print/Copy
Brochure/Booklet	L–M	High	High	Staple/Glue	Moderate	Print
Newsletter	L–M	Moderate	Moderate	Flat/Fold	Moderate	Print/Copy
Magazine/Journal	M–H	Low	Moderate	Staple	High	Print
Newspaper	Mod	Moderate	Moderate	Fold	High	Print
Book/Manual	High	Low	Low	Glue/Mech.	Moderate	Print/Copy
Form/Coupon	Low	High	Low	Flat/Glue	Low	Print
Sign/Poster	Low	Moderate	Moderate	None	Low	Other
Invitation/Menu	Low	Low	Low	None	Low	Print/Copy
Letterhead	Low	Low	Low	None	Low	Print
Envelope/Pack	Low	Low	Low	None	Low	Print
Presentations	L–M	Moderate	High	None	Mod–High	Other

Desktop Typography with QuarkXPress

Creating a page

The genesis of a page lies somewhere in the triangle formed by the needs of the project, the material to be used, and your creative instincts.

Project needs

Although publications may differ in their goals or modus operandi, they usually settle into relatively standardized page dimensions. Since many pieces are reproduced on copying machines and offset duplicators, the page size will be dictated by the sheet-size limitations of the reproduction device. And even though most of these devices can "print" smaller page sizes, most people use the common $8^1/_2 \times 11$ inch cut sheet.

Most newsletters, for example, tend to be $8^1/_2 \times 11$ inches or $8^1/_2 \times 14$ inches or multiples of these sizes—$5^1/_2 \times 8^1/_2$ (half of an $8^1/_2 \times 11$) or $7 \times 8^1/_2$ (half of an $8^1/_2 \times 14$). Page size can be affected by a number of variables—envelope size, the size of the mailing carton, and most of all, budget.

The contents of a publication often force certain page sizes and formats. Detailed drawings or schematics may prohibit smaller page sizes, and voluminous text may dictate a larger page size in order to reduce the number of pages and the bulk of the document.

A combination of project goal (and budget) and anticipated contents will usually determine the general nature of the publication.

The most common page design procedure:

- Page category: Type of job, e.g., newsletter
- Page size: Overall page dimensions
- Page orientation: Portrait or landscape
- Page borders: Top, bottom, left, right
- Page grid: Columnar makeup
- Content definition: Specify content elements

The page grid has been with us longer than printing. Pre-medieval scribes ruled line and column guides on their sheets of vellum, papyrus, and paper in preparation for writing. This allowed them to maintain a consistent appearance for each page with a symmetry and aesthetic that supposedly transcended human appreciation.

The lightly-traced guidelines are still visible on Gutenbergian Bibles, the first work of printing "technology." These lines guided the positioning of columns, margins, folios, and headings. The printing process itself required consistency of positioning, so that the impression of type from the front of a page matched the impression from the rear. Today's processes do not create a strike-through, but the use of lightweight papers causes a "see-through." Thus, aligning page elements (margins, lines, etc.) on the front and back of pages serves a useful purpose.

The most basic page layout consideration involves the borders or margins. Traditionally, the bottom margin was slightly deeper (width is expressed as either wide or narrow, depth is shallow or deep) than the top margin, and the margin adjacent to the gutter or fold was narrower than the other margin.

Because many pages produced with modern technology (laser printing and high speed copier/duplicators) will be single-sided and not bound in traditional forms, many users use a symmetrical border arrangement for all pages. You may change any dimension, of course. Certain page orientations are more appropriate than others.

Make the bottom margin a little bigger than the other three

Desktop Typography with QuarkXPress

Here are the most commonly used page sizes for various print materials. Both Portrait and Landscape versions are indicated:

	$2^3/_4$ ×$4^1/_4$		$5^1/_2$ ×$8^1/_2$		6 ×9		7 ×$8^1/_2$		7 ×10		8 ×10		$8^1/_2$ ×11		$8^1/_2$ ×14		9 ×12		11 ×17		12 ×18	
	P	L	P	L	P	L	P	L	P	L	P	L	P	L	P	L	P	L	P	L	P	L
Book, journal	I	S	F	S	F	S	I	I	F	S	F	S	F	S	S	N	N	N	I	I	I	N
Newsletter, magazine	S	S	I	S	I	S	I	S	S	I	I	S	F	S	F	I	S	I	F	I	S	S
Documentation	I	I	F	S	F	S	S	I	F	S	F	S	F	S	F	I	S	N	S	N	I	I
Catalog, directory	S	S	S	I	F	I	I	I	S	I	F	I	F	I	S	S	S	S	S	S	S	S
Advertising, promo	S	S	I	I	I	I	S	I	F	I	F	I	F	I	I	S	F	S	F	S	F	I
Presentational	S	S	S	S	I	I	I	I	S	S	F	N	F	F	F	S	I	I	S	S	S	S
Utility	F	F	S	S	F	S	S	S	F	S	F	S	F	S	F	S	S	S	F	S	F	S

P Portrait
L Landscape
F Frequently used
S Sometimes used
I Infrequently used
N Never used

Desktop Typography with QuarkXPress

All pages start out with the same underlying framework, which assumes that you would not want to place most page elements flush with the four edges. Using margins creates a border of white space on the page that serves as a "frame." On some book and magazine pages, photos and color blocks extend all the way to the edge to create what is called a "bleed." Laser and other high technology printers may have limitations in producing bleeds if they are sheet fed, because they cannot print to the sheet edge. Usually a bleed is created by using a larger sheet size and then trimming it as required.

The page border is important. It helps to create both a focus for the eye and a consistency as the reader turns from page to page.

Page architecture

A 2-page spread

Outer margin

Running head or header

Live matter area inside the margins

Columns, separated by column gutters. This illustration straddles the columns

2   Running foot or footer   3

Even page number or folio, left hand or verso page

Gutter or inside margin

Odd page number or folio, right hand or rector page

A note on production of this illustration. Using the QuarkXPress text frames, you can build each section. The **Modify** function lets you specify the tint or the solid white. The tweak position as required.

Desktop Typography with QuarkXPress

A page is actually an architectural unit. The outside or finished page dimensions are the frame. The borders then define an actual work or image area. Within the image area there are columns, the size of which varies according to the number of columns and the space between them.

PORTRAIT (Tall)

Finished Size (inches)	Image Area (inches)	1 col	2 col	3 col	4 col	5 col	6 col
$2^3/_4 \times 4^1/_4$	$2^1/_4 \times 3^3/_4$	$2^1/_4$	1	—	—	—	—
$5^1/_2 \times 8^1/_2$	$4^1/_2 \times 7$	$4^1/_2$	2	$1^1/_8$	—	—	—
6×9	$4^1/_2 \times 7^1/_2$	$4^1/_2$	2	$1^1/_8$	—	—	—
$7 \times 8^1/_2$	$5^1/_2 \times 7$	$5^1/_2$	$2^1/_2$	$1^1/_2$	1	—	—
7×10	$5^1/_2 \times 8$	$5^1/_2$	$2^1/_2$	$1^1/_2$	1	—	—
8×10	$6^1/_2 \times 8$	$6^1/_2$	3	$1^3/_4$	$1^1/_4$	—	—
$8^1/_2 \times 11$	7×9	7	$3^1/_4$	2	$1^3/_8$	—	—
$8^1/_2 \times 14$	$6^1/_2 \times 12$	$6^1/_2$	3	$1^3/_4$	$1^1/_4$	—	—
9×12	$7^1/_2 \times 10$	$7^1/_2$	$3^1/_2$	$2^1/_8$	$1^1/_2$	—	—
11×17	9×14	9	$4^1/_4$	$2^3/_4$	2	$1^3/_4$	1
12×18	10×15	10	$4^3/_4$	3	$2^1/_4$	$1^3/_4$	$1^1/_4$

LANDSCAPE (Wide)

Image Area (inches)	1 col	2 col	3 col	4 col	5 col	6 col
$3^3/_4 \times 2^1/_4$	$3^3/_4$	$1^3/_4$	—	—	—	—
$7 \times 4^1/_2$	7	$3^1/_4$	2	$1^1/_8$	—	—
$7^1/_2 \times 4^1/_2$	$7^1/_2$	$3^1/_2$	2	$1^1/_8$	—	—
$7 \times 5^1/_2$	7	$3^1/_4$	2	$1^3/_8$	—	—
$8 \times 5^1/_2$	8	$3^3/_4$	$2^1/_4$	$1^3/_4$	1	—
$8 \times 6^1/_2$	8	$3^3/_4$	$2^1/_4$	$1^3/_4$	—	—
9×7	9	$4^1/_4$	$2^3/_4$	2	$1^3/_4$	1
$12 \times 6^1/_2$	12	$5^3/_4$	3	2	$1^3/_4$	1
12×9	12	$5^3/_4$	3	2	$1^3/_4$	1
14×9	14	$6^3/_4$	$3^1/_2$	$2^1/_4$	$1^3/_4$	$1^1/_4$
15×10	15	$7^1/_4$	$3^1/_2$	$2^1/_4$	$1^3/_4$	$1^1/_4$

Desktop Typography with QuarkXPress

Columns

Next, the number of columns and their width is specified. As space is taken away from the column width, it is usually distributed to the gutters or margins.

1 column = 7"
2 columns = $3^1/_4$" each
3 columns = 2" each
4 columns = $1^3/_8$" each
2 of the 2 columns = $4^1/_2$"
2 of the 4 columns = $3^1/_8$"
3 of the 4 columns = $4^1/_8$"

A page column grid can be as flexible or as rigid as you desire. A two-column layout, for example, can keep all content items at the one-column width, even illustrations. Or, the column widths can be combined to create areas of emphasis or separation. For example, a basic four-column grid can be modified by setting type two or three columns wide and leaving some white space. In the list above, the four column grid has been broken for one area two columns wide and another area three columns wide.

In some four-column layouts the first column is left blank to create a slightly asymmetrical look. The white space can be used for gloss, notes, etc.

The process of putting pages together is both a creative and a production process. Someone, somewhere in the workflow must determine the overall format of the page based upon the following basic parameters:

- number of columns
- width of columns
- size of gutters and margins
- typeface size and interline spacing
- paragraph style—indents or not
- position and size of illustrations
- style and position of running heads and feet, and page numbers
- style of captions, callouts, and footnotes
- overall typographic look: justified, ragged, letterspaced negatively or positively.

Columnar alternatives

The four-column format is most popular because it accommodates the sizes of advertisements. Publications that do not have the problem of accommodating ads should develop other patterns. White space can be used as a design element. For instance, narrower columns can be concentrated toward the center of the spread, creating a wide outer margin that can be used for headlines or illustrations. Or use two columns and center them down the middle of the page, giving them ample outer margins to create a dignified feeling.

Consider using three columns per page but making them narrower than the maximum. You then have the option of placing them in two positions on the page: working outward from the gutter, yielding a wide outer margin; or working inward from the outer edge, yielding a wide gutter margin. The advantage of an unusual arrangement is that it makes the page "feel" different. The framework to which you attach your material forces you to size it according to certain proportions. If the framework is ordinary, your page proportions will also be ordinary. If it is unusual, then the result will look unusual.

Mixing column widths on the same page creates a variety in look and scale as well as in emphasis. A change in pattern helps to fragment the large page into component parts at first glance. This optical division depends on a horizontal building-block makeup: instead of snaking copy from column to column, each item takes up a small rectangle of space on the page, defined by the columns themselves. The top and bottom edges are defined by alignment of the type and by the headline that is placed across the top. The space between such rectangles acts as a separating gutter if its edges are precise and straight. You can add cut-off rules, if you feel the need for them.

Sidebars

Sidebars are special text areas that contain material related to the accompanying text. Sidebar type is set in boxes that are often ruled, outlined, or tinted with black or colored ink. Be careful to set the text of a sidebar narrower than the regular column width so that there is space between the type and the graphic (rule) that surrounds it. Sidebars should be coordinated with the column structure. Pay attention to the relationship between the headline type used with regular text and the reduced heads in sidebars.

Sidebars can be disturbing elements. Think of them as graphics—nonpictorial pattern breakers. Anything that breaks a pattern attracts attention. Make sure you use a typeface of contrasting size, color, and texture.

Chapter 19

Aspects of Design

Desktop Typography with QuarkXPress

Romano's Rules for Layout

1. Be consistent.

Handle the various elements of graphic design on each page and within a publication consistently. Use the same margins throughout the publication. If some of your headlines are set center, all headlines should be set centered. Do not change typeface or size abruptly or without good reason.

2. Avoid dullness.

Too much balance and symmetry can lead to boredom. Interrupted eye movement occurs when the reader's eyes are faced with equal-sized elements. Tension or asymmetry adds interest to a page. Unequal left–right or top–bottom balance helps provide movement.

3. Each page should have a dominant visual element.

Provide a focal point and a resting spot for the reader's eyes before they begin their travel through the page.

4. Design facing pages.

In most instances, pages are viewed two at a time. Concentrate your design efforts on two-page spreads and create pages that work together. But don't try to run copy across the fold unless you are in the center spread.

5. Create a grid.

A grid consists of nonprinting horizontal and vertical lines that define the placement of graphic elements that make up a page. They form a publication's overall organization and consistency.

6. Standardize margins.

Indent copy, headlines, titles, and page numbers the same distance from top, bottom, and sides of all pages unless you are dealing with a spread.

7. Use borders as frames.

Frame your pages with appropriate borders.

8. Organize text into columns.

Select column widths appropriate to the size of type. Use wide columns for large type sizes. Use narrow columns for small type sizes.

Desktop Typography with QuarkXPress

9. Organize the page with horizontal or vertical rules.
Rule weight should depend on how it relates to the copy and white space. Use vertical rules to separate columns. Use horizontal rules to separate topics within a column. Be careful about using rules and boxes together.

10. Create sign posts.
Headers (running heads) refer to information contained at the top of each page. Page numbers may be placed in the header or footer (running feet).

11. Use type with personality.
Each typeface evokes a different feeling, speaks in a different tone of voice. The typefaces you select for headlines, subheads, body copy, and captions affect the way readers experience your ideas. Use only a few but make them count.

12. Provide a strong flag.
The flag is your publication's title set in a unique way. The flag is usually the dominant visual element on the first page of a publication.

13. Use dominant, descriptive headlines.
Headlines contribute to the overall appearance by strengthening the message you want to communicate. Headlines should be large but must not compete with other page elements.

14. Let subheads provide transition.
Subheads direct readers into the body copy. Subheads also break up long blocks of copy. Subheads make it easy to locate information. Subheads are good.

15. Use captions to describe photographs and artwork.
Captions should be set in smaller type so they do not compete with the body copy.

16. Use color to set elements apart.
Use color to highlight borders, rules, and headlines. Color gains impact when it is used selectively.

17. Use big type to emphasize big ideas.
Type size should reflect importance. Headlines should be larger than subheads. Subheads should be larger than body copy, and body copy should be larger than captions and footnotes.

18. Use type styles for emphasis.
Add emphasis to copy by setting headlines, subheads, and body copy in different typefaces, but check out Rules 1 and 11 first.

19. Use white space as a page element.
White space emphasizes whatever it surrounds. Frame pages with white space to focus attention. Let your page breathe.

20. Use tints and reverses for attention.
Screen tints and reverses can be used to add interest to pages without photographs or illustrations.

21. Define text or graphics with boxes.
Use boxes to define elements, but don't overdo it.

22. Focus ideas with graphics.
Use photographs, illustrations, charts, and graphs to communicate ideas at a glance and add visual variety. Crop photos for emphasis.

23. Check text and layout.
Always check your work. Make sure that nothing important has been left out. Check names, addresses, and phone numbers. Check for graphic consistency and accuracy. Then, double-check.

Even more layout

Desktop Typography with QuarkXPress

Copy elements

The following is a list of the main elements of most documents and publications. A two-letter mnemonic is also provided. This approach is also called "generic coding," since it defines copy elements by their final form. This list may help you in establishing a set of typographic definitions for each element so that all personnel involved in publishing know the specifications for each copy block that appears on your pages.

Origination
BY	Byline
PO	Position or TI for Title
AF	Affiliation
CP	Colophon

Titling
CT	Cover Title
OT	Opening Title
ST	Section Title
TT	Table Title
RT	Running Title

Introductory Data
EX	Explanation
IN	Introduction
AB	Abstract

Text
TX	Text
T1...	Levels of Text
FL	First Line of Text
LI	Lists of Text
ML	Multi-Column List
OU	Outline
TA	Table

Heading
HD	Head
H1...	Levels of Head (Subheads)
SH	Section (Chapter) Head
TN	Table Number
CH	Column Head
RH	Running Head

Peripheral Text
CA	Caption
CR	Credit

CO   Callout
NO   Note
MF   Math Formula

Directional

TC   Table of Contents
IN   Index
BB   Bibliography
GL   Glossary
AP   Appendix

Other

FO   Folio
BO   Box
RL   Rule Line
TI   Tint
CH   Chart
IL   Illustration
GR   Graph
HC   Highlight Color

The following are some of the traditional rules governing pages: **Pages**

1. Typographic widows and orphans should be avoided. A widow is text less than one third of a full line wide at the end of a paragraph. An orphan is a widow as the first line at the top of a column.

2. Pages that are not full length, such as at the ends of sections and chapters, should have at least four or five lines of text.

3. Facing pages may be a line long or a line short to avoid bad breaks. However, facing pages should be the same length, and long pages should not back up short pages.

4. A heading should not be the last line on a page. A headline should have at least two lines of text below it. If this isn't possible, carry it over to the next page.

5. A page may run short if otherwise a heading would fall at the bottom of the page.

6. Right-hand pages should not end with a hyphen if possible.

Desktop Typography with QuarkXPress

7. Pages should not end with a colon, and at least two lines should follow a colon at the bottom of a page. In cases in which only three lines follow the colon, put one at the bottom of the page and two at the top of the next page.

8. When footnotes are placed at the bottom of a page, they are set apart from the text by a blank line, a short rule, or a full-width rule. On a short page at the end of a chapter, the note follows the text with the same space intervening; in other words, it is not dropped to the foot of the page.

9. Running heads and folios should be deleted from a page containing only a table or an illustration.

Headings

Headings are breaks in the text, like billboards on a highway, that introduce or flag the subject matter that follows. Headline type should stand out from the text in size and, usually, in weight. The size of the headline depends on the length of the text and on its relationship to other visual elements. Short texts should usually have smaller headline sizes than long texts.

If there is only one headline on a relatively small page, a smaller size is appropriate. If there are many headlines and text areas (as one might see in newspapers and newsletters), the headlines compete with other elements. Any main headlines should be distinctive.

The purpose of headlines is to attract the attention of the reader and indicate the content of the text that follows.

The length of the text should determine the size of the headline and the number of lines it can take. Short texts require smaller headline sizes than long texts. Multi-column heads are usually larger than single-column ones.

Research into legibility suggests that headlines should be set flush left, not centered, because the eyes are conditioned to the reference point on the left. The heads should not be "blocked out" (that is, fill the line) but should have a bit of white space at the end of the line. Leading between headlines should be at a minimum because space is usually already built in by the typeface's ascenders and descenders.

Desktop Typography with QuarkXPress

Simplicity in design dictates that only a few typefaces should be mixed together. Using too many faces leads to visual confusion. It is good to go for strong visual contrast. Hence, an effective (and often used) combination of faces is serif text and sans serif headlines. Typeface groups that are very similar should not be mixed because the contrast will be weak.

Transitional, Old Style, and Modern typefaces are similar and, therefore, don't contrast well. But sans serif and square serifs do make for good contrast with those three groups because of their pronounced differences.

When it comes to text type, the primary concern is legibility. Headlines, on the other hand, may be more colorful, expressing the content more liberally.

Heads are designed to stand out from the main text. There are many techniques used to achieve this, such as larger type size, bold or italic type, caps and small caps, etc. "Style" refers to the way the head is set, rather than the typeface or position on the page. The following styles may be specified:

Heads

    clc — caps and lowercase (each major word has an initial cap)
    ulc — upper and lowercase (initial cap on the first word only)
    caps — all capital letters
    c/sc — caps and small caps

1. In a cap heading, en dashes should be used for hyphens, and space between words should be the minimum word space.

2. Avoid dividing words in headings.

3. A centered head that can be set in less than three full lines should be arranged in an inverted pyramid style, each line centered and shorter than the line above it. A longer heading may be set in block style — that is, each line justified and the last line centered.

4. Running heads should not go over one line, allowing at least an em space between the head and folio. Running heads are more common than running feet.

Lists and tables | The following are guidelines for setting lists in columns:

1. If an uneven number of items are to be set in two columns, the first column may be one line longer than the second.

Item 1	**Item 2**
Item 3	**Item 4**
Item 5	**Item 6**
Item 7	

If the number of items to be set in three columns is one item short of being a multiple of three, the first two columns should be one line longer than the third.

Item 1	**Item 2**	**Item 3**
Item 4	**Item 5**	**Item 6**
Item 7	**Item 8**	

If the number is one more than a multiple of three, the first or second columns should include one more item than the other two columns.

2. A simple two-column tabulation should be indented on both sides so that the individual columns are not too wide. A long narrow list should be set in two columns.

3. Each entry in tabular columns must align horizontally with the entry in the stub to which it refers. (The stub is the area at the left that has descriptive copy in it.) When the stub entry is several lines long, alignment is with the bottom line of the stub entry; if column entries are also several lines long, all first lines align.

4. Carryover lines of stub entries are indented nine units (or one pica) under the first line. The word "total" should be indented more than any other line in the stub.

5. A column of words or dissimilar items may be centered or aligned at the left. Short items are better centered; longer items should be aligned at left.

6. In vertical alignment, columns of whole numbers are aligned on the right or aligned at the decimal points. Plus, minus, and equal signs should be aligned.

Dollar and percentage signs should be aligned. In a column in which all numbers denote either dollars or percentages consistently, the signs are used with the first numbers in the columns and after every break, such as a rule or a heading.

7. Table captions. If tables are set in two or three different type sizes in order to accommodate them to the measure of the document, the captions should all be in one size.

8. Column heads. In an unruled table, headings are set so that they align across the bottom and are centered over the columns to which they refer.

This	**This**	
is a	is a	**This**
head	head	is a

In a ruled table all columns are centered horizontally and vertically in the boxes allotted to them.

9. Continued tables. If a table is more than one page in length, the table number and caption should be repeated at the top of each page, followed by the word "continued."

The column heads should be repeated if a table continues on another page. The table number and column heads of a wide table set broadside (landscape) on the page need only be repeated on the left-hand pages.

10. Broadside (now called landscape) tables are positioned so that they read properly when rotated a quarter turn to the right (heads at the left of the page).

11. If leaders, em dashes, or blanks are used to indicate no data available for a particular line, the dollar sign is placed before the first number in the column, not at the top of the column.

12. If the numbers in a column do not all denote dollars or percent, the dollar or percent sign should be used with every one that does.

Subheads

In a text in which the chapters are long and the material is complicated, the author (or the editor) may insert subheadings in the text as guides for the reader. Subheads should be kept short, succinct, and meaningful. Like chapter titles, subheads should be similar in sense and tone.

Many publications require only one degree (level) of subhead throughout the text. Some technical works, for example, require sub-subheads and even further subdivisions. When more than one degree of subhead is used, the subheads are referred to as the A-level subhead (the principal subhead), the B-level subhead (the secondary subhead), the C-level, and so on. Only in the most complicated works does the need for more than three levels arise. Examples:

A-level Head
B-Level Head
C-Level Head

Subheads, except the lowest level, are each set on a line separate from the text. The levels are differentiated by type and placement. The lowest level is often set at the beginning of a paragraph in italics and followed by a period. This type of subhead is referred to as a run-in head.

In technical publishing, however, the numbering of sections, subsections, and sometimes sub-subsections makes for easy reference and may be a real convenience to the reader. There are various ways to number sections. The most common method is the double numeration system, in which the number of a section consists of the number of the chapter, a decimal point, and the number of the section within a chapter. The number 6.6, for example, signifies the sixth section in chapter 6. A subsection might be numbered 6.6.1.

In addition to display pages in the front matter, running heads are usually omitted from part titles, chapter openings, and any page containing only an illustration or a table. A running head should be used on any page containing both an illustration (or a table) and lines of text.

Sample page

A sample page should contain all the variables you can foresee in the document or publication. The variables should be considered for the draft printout as well as the proof or final result. A sample page or page should contain:

> Left and right running heads
> Left and right running footers
> Page numbers and their position
> Footnotes
> Section or chapter heads

Main heads
Subheads
Typographic emphasis
Use of italic or underline
Captions or call-outs
Treatment of formulae
Tabular format
Numbers of lines on a page

Creating a style sheet and sample pages will aid in preparing copy whenever there is more than one person entering that copy. Any questions you have while you are creating the style and sample sheets will surely come up with other operators. Solve page problems early and avoid frustrating situations that may occur later in the production cycle.

Considers in copy preparation or authoring:

Authoring

1. Use the figure 1 for the numeral one.

2. Don't use the lowercase letter l for the numeral one.

3. Do not use the letter o for a zero.

4. Use consistent vertical spacing throughout the document.

5. Consistently start and end each paragraph with the same indent or spacing sequence.

6. Use automatic word-wrap (which automatically begins a new line when the word is longer than the available space) throughout your document.

7. Use hard returns (actually press the return key) where required—heads, subheads, and paragraph endings.

8. Avoid using hyphenation for information that will be transported to the publishing system.

9. Underlining—depending on the word processing software being used—should be avoided.

10. Provide a printout of the document and directory of the disk for documents to be converted or typeset.

11. If heads and subheads are to be either all caps or initial capped, type them the same way they are to appear.

12. Try to consistently identify each element within the document.

13. Place footnotes at the end of the document and number them sequentially.

14. Make a backup copy of your document.

15. Produce a backup disk.

16. Understand your word processor's ability to convert your document to a transportable ASCII file.

Desktop Typography with QuarkXPress

Consider some of these items when beginning or preparing information for publishing:

Layout
Running heads
Running footers
Page numbering
Section numbering
Illustrations
Positioning of illustrations
Space between running heads and first head line
Space between running heads and first text line
Space between last text line and bottom margin
Space between last text line and bottom page number
Space above a major head
Space between a major head and a subhead
Space before a subhead
Space after a subhead
Space between paragraphs
Space above a footnote
Space between a footnote and a page number
Space between a footnote and the bottom margin
Left margin
Right margin
Gutters
Tabular formats
Font usage
Point size usage

Desktop Typography with QuarkXPress

Other elements

Logo, nameplate, flag, banner, and masthead: *Logos* in Greek means word. When each character was cast separately as a piece of metal and words had to be assembled individually into lines, commonly used character combinations were made into single units to save compositor's time. Such pre-set units were called logotypes. The name was then transferred to any image that was specially prepared and repeated, such as company or trade names. This usage was then applied to the name of the publication. A publication's title is a nameplate, or a flag, or banner. Logo is commonly used for magazines; nameplate for newsletters; banner or flag for tabloids. Do not call the name of the publication the *masthead* because that term is used for the list of individuals responsible for the publication.

æ   œ

Logotype

Logo

𝕿𝖍𝖊 𝕹𝖊𝖜 𝖄𝖔𝖗𝖐 𝕿𝖎𝖒𝖊𝖘

Flag

Decks and blurbs: Headlines may be accompanied by a deck, which is several lines of display type that expand the meaning of the headline or explain its significance. Since one thought flows from the previous one, it is logical to place the elements in a like manner: headline at the top, deck beneath it, text below the deck. Decks are also often called blurbs.

Heading!

Deck below

Deck above

Heading!

Captions, legends, cutlines: Captions, legends, and cutlines are used as openers to a story, for instance, the headline that is seen near them takes the place of the caption and does the work of focusing the interpretation of the picture in its own words.

Catch lines and boldface lead-ins: Catch lines are usually written as labels—self-contained and free-standing. Boldface lead-ins depend on typographic contrast, with the first words of the first sentence set either bolder, all caps, larger, or in a contrasting face to the rest of the text. The words set in bold should be worthy of such emphasis.

Pull quotes: These are quotes taken from the copy and inserted as a graphic element in the text column. In many cases, the use of pull quotes is designed to fill up space so that the text will align within the columns neatly.

Style sheets: Some page formats can be established once and stored as page grids or style files for repetitive use. In other words, the creative process may only be necessary once; after that, production personnel can follow the format, especially if the printed material flows from page to page without interruption. If, however, there are numerous interruptions to the text flow, such as illustrations, then creative involvement may be necessary.

Just as there are page elements that act as building blocks for pages, pages themselves are building blocks for other entities: documents and publications.

Captions

Desktop Typography with QuarkXPress

Suggestions for designing with type

1. Before you start any design project, always ask these questions: What is it for? Who's going to read it? Under what reading conditions? Who will care about what you will do?

2. How will be it printed? On what stock? The limitations of the reproduction process often mandate certain design approaches.

3. In order to break rules, you must learn the rules first. In order to do something new, you must know what has been done before. Publishing can be philosophical, as you can see.

4. A good design is always a simple design.

5. It's not the typeface that counts; it's how a typeface is used that matters.

6. You cannot salvage a bad idea with a good execution. For instance, reversing very thin type on textured stock is not a good idea.

7. Study your copy carefully—sounds, letter combinations, meaning, tone of voice, etc. Many ideas and design solutions evolve from playing with words.

8. Don't be satisfied too quickly. If you think you have the problem solved, put the idea aside and try something else, something totally different. Never become too satisfied.

9. Don't just study good design, study bad design, too (there is enough around). Find out what bothers you, why it doesn't work. In other words, learn from other people's mistakes.

10. There are no bad typefaces (except for Souvenir). There is only bad usage of type.

11. Be objective. Pretend you are the audience. Look at your design from this point of view. What do you want them to do? What action should someone take?

12. Try de-design. Delete any design element that doesn't contribute to the strength of your basic idea. Keep deleting until everything on the page has a reason to be there.

13. Type puts clothes on words. Words express ideas. If you want to be good with type, you have to respect words and appreciate ideas first.

Don't be afraid to use rules, screens, bullets, and boxes to call attention to and emphasize important facts in your manuals. Most people merely skim a manual for information — it's rare for someone to read a manual cover to cover. For that reason, you need to emphasize levels of importance. And don't forget that the publications you produce are a direct interface between your readers and the company you represent.

As with other publications, try to establish consistent graphic standards in manual production.

Chapter 20

A Little Graphics

Desktop Typography with QuarkXPress

Some aspects of graphics work hand-in-hand with typography. These include:

- Tints
- Rules
- Boxes
- Borders

Tints are essentially dot or halftone patterns that cover a defined area. Tints are used with text to emphasize the material or to set it apart from other copy on the page.

 QuarkXPress lets you specify tints in percentages from 0% to 100% in 1 point increments. Users with color monitors also have the option of creating shades in color.

This feature allows you to fill any text box with a background tint. To shade a text box, activate the box and select **Modify** from the **Item** menu. In the **Shade** text field, enter a value between between 1 and 100 (a 0 percent screen leaves the background white).

The tints at left can also be specified in color. Black, Blue, Cyan, Green, Magenta, Red or Yellow are available, or you can create custom colors.

When using shaded text boxes, be careful not to make the background too dark. As a general rule, don't use screens darker that 50 percent with black type. Any boxes darker than 50 percent black require white type.

The use of white type with a dark background is called a reverse. To create white type against a shaded background in QuarkXPress, highlight the type you want to be white and select **Color** from the **Style** menu. From the pop-up menu, select **White.**

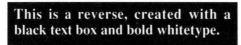

This is a reverse, created with a black text box and bold whitetype.

Desktop Typography with QuarkXPress

For the best reproduction, a 10 percent shade works best as a background for type. Heavier and bold typefaces are easiest to read when covered by a tint; avoid typefaces with fine serifs.

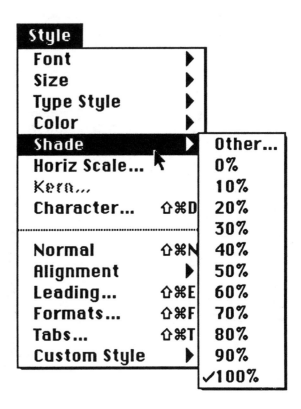

The Shade pop-up menu

Boxes

Boxes are simply rule lines that meet at the corners. In QuarkXPress, you use the **Frame** command under the **Item** menu to create rules around text boxes. You can choose from 17 styles of frames—from simple to complex and from hairline width to as wide as the box will allow.

To create a border around a text box, activate the box and from the **Item** menu, select **Frame**. Enter a value in the **Size** text field (enter 0.25 for a hairline rule, 1 pt for a one point rule, etc). If you want something other than a plain frame, select one from the list. You can also specify color.

A border should work with the text that encloses it. That is, a sans serif face should have a simple border; serif fonts should have more ornate borders. Actually, it makes no real difference, as long as the type and the border don't clash.

Desktop Typography with QuarkXPress

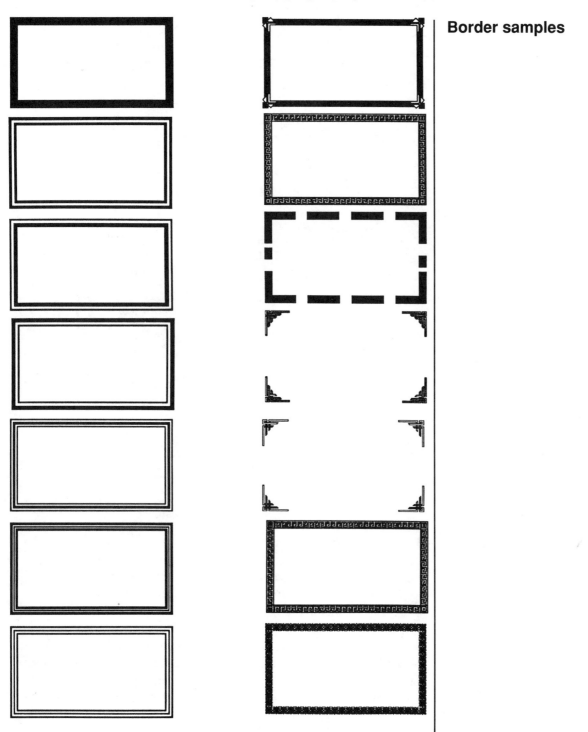

Border samples

These are 14 of the 17 borders that available in QuarkXpress. You can also use the Frame Editor to create border styles.

Desktop Typography with QuarkXPress

Using frames

Usually a simple one-point rule is the best border for a boxed area. You may wish to try different frame weights (line thicknesses) to arrive at the one that appears best. Here are two frames:

Framed at 1 point   **Framed at 12 points**

A border that is too heavy overpowers the box.

You can create a drop shadow effect by making one text box solid black (select **Modify** under the **Item** menu; enter 100 in the **Shade** text field; make sure Black is the selected color). The top text box has a 1 point rule around it.

If text is to run-around the box, you may wish to specify a small indent to create some white space between the box and the text. For the example above, .01" was used as a left indent.

Rule lines

Rule lines can be used to highlight text or to set blocks of text off from one another.

———————————————————————

The rule above adds emphasis to this sentence
as well as this block of text.

QuarkXPress gives you a wide range of choices when creating rules. Rules can be drawn at any angle (and text can be run-around for a graphic effect). and can contain arrowheads on one end or both. Color and shade can also be specified.

For simple coupon rules you might find the **Shift-Hyphen** (baseline rule) works fastest. You can even go to a different point size to make the rule lighter.

Name_____
Firm_____
At 12-point, same as text

The only problem is that the rules may not align at their ends (especially in ragged text) depending on the amount of text on the line. You can solve this by using a tab setting with the **Hyphen-Shift** underline character as a fill character. You can also try the old photo-typesetting trick of putting a word space between the rules and the text and then justifying the lines:

Style menu choices for rules

Of course, you can use QuarkXPress's line creation tool to insert horizontal, vertical and angled rule lines anywhere.

Once again, weight is important. It is best to keep rules around 1 point in width so that they do not overwhelm the text or other elements on the page.

You can also make a heavier rule less obnoxious by shading them. The rule above has a 20 percent shade.

Use all of these graphics approaches sparingly.

Desktop Typography with QuarkXPress

Other sources

"Automated Typesetting—The Basic Course," Frank Romano, 1974, GAMA, Salem, NH

"Directory of Evocative Typography," Renee LeWinter, 1980, GAMA, Salem, NH

"Illustrated Handbook of Desktop Publishing and Typesetting," Michael Kleper, 1987, TAB Books, Blue Ridge Summit, PA

"International Paper Pocket Pal," 1987, Michael Bruno and Frank Romano

"Machine Writing and Typesetting," Frank Romano, 1986, GAMA, Salem, NH

"The Type Encyclopedia," Frank Romano, 1986, R.R. Bowker, New York, NY

"Type Design Developments," 1970–1985, L.W. Wallis, 1985, GAMA, Salem, NH

"Types and Typefaces," J. Ben Liberman, 1978, Myriade Press, New Rochelle, NY

"Typography: How to make it most legible," Rolf Rehe, 1974, Design Research International, Carmel, IN

"Words into Type," 3rd Edition 1974, Prentice Hall, Ft Lee, NJ

A free catalog of these books and others on typography is available from TypeWorld, P.O. Box 170, Salem, NH 03079.

Short-Cut Keyboard Commands

About QuarkXPress (help)..........⌘-? *or* ⌘-/

File
New.. ⌘-N
Open.. ⌘-O
Save .... ⌘-S
Get Text/Picture................................. ⌘-E
Page Setup.............................. ⌘-Option-P
Print... ⌘-P
Transfer... ⌘-T
Quit .... ⌘-Q

Edit
Undo.. ⌘-Z
Cut... ⌘-X
Copy... ⌘-C
Paste .... ⌘-V
Select All... ⌘-A
Find/Change .... ⌘-F
Preferences .... ⌘-Y

Style (for Text)
Size
  Other.. ⌘-Shift-\
Type Style
  Plain Text.................................. ⌘-Shift-P
  Bold.. ⌘-Shift-B
  Italic... ⌘-Shift-I
  Underline .... ⌘-Shift-U
  Word Underline........................ ⌘-Shift-W
  Strike Thru .... ⌘-Shift-/
  Outline...................................... ⌘-Shift-O
  Shadow...................................... ⌘-Shift-S
  All Caps..................................... ⌘-Shift-K
  Small Caps .... ⌘-Shift-H
  Superscript................................ ⌘-Shift-+
  Subscript .... ⌘-Shift-hyphen
Character .... ⌘-Shift-D
Normal.................................... ⌘-Shift-N

Style (for Text), cont.
Alignment
  Left .... ⌘-Shift-L
  Centered .... ⌘-Shift-C
  Right .... ⌘-Shift-R
  Justified .... ⌘-Shift-J
Leading .... ⌘-Shift-E
Formats .... ⌘-Shift-F
Tabs....................................... ⌘-Shift-T

Style (for Pictures)
Negative .... ⌘-Shift-hyphen
Normal Contrast .... ⌘-Shift-N
High Contrast .... ⌘-Shift-H
Posterized Contrast...................... ⌘-Shift-P
Other Contrast .... ⌘-Shift-C
Other Screen................................. ⌘-Shift-S

Style (for Lines)
Width
  Other .... ⌘-Shift-\

Item
Modify................................... ⌘-M
Frame.................................... ⌘-B
Duplicate............................... ⌘-D
Step and Repeat .... ⌘-Option-D
Delete.................................... ⌘-K
Lock .... ⌘-L

Page
Go to Page............................. ⌘-G

View
Show/Hide Rulers............................. ⌘-R
Show/Hide Invisibles .... ⌘-I

Utilities
Check Word .... ⌘-W
Suggested Hyphenation .... ⌘-H

Desktop Typography with QuarkXPress

For Use with Text

Font Size

Increase font size:
Preset range .... ⌘-Shift->
In increments of 1 pt. .... ⌘-Option-Shift->

Decrease font size:
Preset range .... ⌘-Shift-<
In increments of 1 pt. .... ⌘-Option-Shift-<

Leading

Increase leading:
In increments of 1 pt. .... ⌘-Shift-"
In increments
of 1/10 pt. .... ⌘-Option-Shift-"

Decrease leading:
In increments of 1 pt. .... ⌘-Shift-:
In increments
of 1/10 pt. .... ⌘-Option-Shift-:

Kerning/Tracking

Increase Kern/Track amount:
By 10/200 em-space .... ⌘-Shift-}
By 1/200 em-space......... ⌘-Option-Shift-}

Decrease Kern/Track amount:
By 10/200 em-space .... ⌘-Shift-{
By 1/200 em-space......... ⌘-Option-Shift-{

Horizontal Scaling

Horizontal scale amount:
Increase by 5% .... ⌘-]
Decrease by 5% .... ⌘-[

To enter one Symbol Font character

Symbol Font character .... ⌘-Shift-Q

Moving the Insertion Point

Move to:
Previous character .... ←
Next character .... →
Previous line .... ↑
Next line .... ↓
Previous word .... ⌘-←
Next word .... ⌘-→
Previous paragraph .... ⌘-↑
Next paragraph .... ⌘-↓
Start of the line .... ⌘-Option-←
End of the line .... ⌘-Option-→
Start of the story .... ⌘-Option-↑
End of the story .... ⌘-Option-↓

Extending the Text Selection

To select:
Previous character .... Shift-←
Next character .... Shift-→
Previous line .... Shift-↑
Next line .... Shift-↓
Previous word .... ⌘-Shift-←
Next word .... ⌘-Shift-→
Previous paragraph .... ⌘-Shift-↑
Next paragraph .... ⌘-Shift-↓
Start of line..................... ⌘-Option-Shift-←
End of line..................... ⌘-Option-Shift-→
Start of story .... ⌘-Option-Shift-↑
End of story .... ⌘-Option-Shift-↓

Deletions

To delete:
Previous character........................... Delete
Next character .... Shift-Delete
Previous word............................. ⌘-Delete
Next word .... ⌘-Shift-Delete
Selected text .... Delete
Selected boxes and lines .... ⌘-K

Desktop Typography with QuarkXPress

Special Characters

New Paragraph, Line, Column, Box

New paragraph .... Return
New line .... Shift-Return
New column.. Enter
New box .... Shift-Enter

Page Numbering

Page number:
  Of the previous text box .... ⌘-2
  Of the current text box .... ⌘-3
  Of the next text box .... ⌘-4

Hyphens

Non-breaking standard hyphen .... ⌘-=
Non-breaking
  short hyphen.................... Option-hyphen
Non-breaking
  long hyphen............ Option-Shift-hyphen
Discretionary (soft) hyphen .... ⌘-hyphen

Spaces

Breaking standard space .... space
Breaking en-space .... Option-space
Breaking standard hyphen............. hyphen
Non-breaking standard space .... ⌘-space
Non-breaking en-space..... ⌘-Option-space

For Use with Pictures

Scaling Pictures

In 5% increments:
  Increase........................... ⌘-Option-Shift->
  Decrease .... ⌘-Option-Shift-<

Centering Pictures

To center .... ⌘-Shift-M
To fit exactly to a box .... ⌘-Shift-F
To fit to a box (maintaining
  aspect ratio)..................... ⌘-Option-Shift-F

For Use with Lines

Line Width

Increase line width:
  Preset range .... ⌘-Shift->
  In increments of 1 pt. .... ⌘-Option-Shift->

Decrease line width:
  Preset range .... ⌘-Shift-<
  In increments of 1 pt. .... ⌘-Option-Shift-<

For Use in Dialog Boxes

OK (or highlighted button)......... Return *or* Enter
Cancel .... ⌘-.
Apply... ⌘-A
Yes .... ⌘-Y
No... ⌘-N
Select next field .... Tab
Select field containing
  insertion bar .... Double-click
Cut .... ⌘-X
Copy .... ⌘-C
Paste .... ⌘-V
In most dialog boxes:
  Undo .... ⌘-Z

Desktop Typography with QuarkXPress

Commands with Keyboard and Mouse

Switching to Different Views

Any view-Actual Size............. Option-click
Actual Size-Fit in Window..... Option-click
Any view-200% .... ⌘-Option-click
200%-Actual Size................ ⌘-Option-click

Resizing Pictures

Constrain* .... Shift-Drag
Maintain
    aspect ratio .... Option-Shift-Drag
Scale picture
    and constrain* .... ⌘-Shift-Drag
Scale picture and maintain
    aspect ratio .... ⌘-Option-Shift-Drag
    * Constrains box to square, oval to circle,
      line to 0°/45°/90°

Clicking to Select Text

Positions insertion point.............. One click
Selects the word .... Two clicks
Selects the line .... Three clicks
Selects the paragraph .... Four clicks
Selects all of the current chain .. Five clicks

Moving Items Without the Mover Tool

Moving items
    With no constraints....................... ⌘-Drag
    With horizontal/vertical
      constraints ....⌘-Shift-Drag

For Use with Rulers

To delete
    ruler guides .... Option-click on ruler

For Use with Tool Palette

To keep
    a tool selected............. Option-click on tool

Removing All Tabs

Remove all tabs ... Option-click on tab ruler

Copying Paragraph Formats

Copy formats
    to selection..................... Shift-Option-click

For the Apple Extended Keyboard

Invoke help module................................. help
Delete next character................................ del
Start of document................................. home
End of document .... end
Scroll up one screen.......................... page up
Scroll down one screen.............. page down
First page...................................... Shift-home
Last page.. Shift-end
Previous page .... Shift-page up
Next page........................... Shift-page down

Index

Index